CW00673451

GROWING
ON
PURPOSE

GROWING ON PURPOSE

STRATEGIC CLARITY *for* PURPOSE-DRIVEN LEADERS

DAVID PATERSON

© 2023

All rights reserved. No part of this book may be reproduced in any form or by any means—whether electronic, digital, mechanical, or otherwise—without permission in writing from the publisher, except by a reviewer, who may quote brief passages in a review.

Hardcover ISBN: 978-0-6458995-0-4
Paperback ISBN: 978-0-6458995-1-1
eBook ISBN: 978-0-6458995-2-8

Scripture quotations marked AMP are from the Amplified Version and are copyright © 2015 by The Lockman Foundation, La Habra, CA 90631. All rights reserved.

Scripture quotations marked CEV are from the Common English Version and are copyright © 1995 by American Bible Society For more information about CEV, visit www.bibles.com and www.cev.bible.

Publisher: Cornerstone Strategic Pty Ltd

To the One whose ways are far higher than my own.

CONTENTS

PREFACE

This book is for leaders engaged in the pursuit of a worthwhile purpose. It is for those who want to make a real difference through the very core of what we do in our roles and organizations, and not just occasionally or on the fringes. It is for those seeking to break through tough societal challenges. It is for those who want to play their part in setting things right in their particular spheres of influence - and in the process create new value, growth and sustainability for their enterprises or communities, whether in the public or private sector or in a start-up or multinational organization.

This book is for those who want to see change in any one of the thousand shifts our beautiful-but-broken world needs to make such as in the domains of social and economic justice, health, education, housing, child protection, poverty reduction, climate change, the environment, and the like.

It's easy to be idealistic about the possibilities when we're first setting out in a new role or on a new project. But as we step further into the real world, we find ourselves pressing through a jungle of conflicting demands and constraints. Add to that an accelerating pace of change in the world around us and our days can easily be consumed by the operationally urgent, leaving precious little time to focus on the strategically vital. It's hard to see the forest for the trees when we're so busy putting out spot fires.

Perhaps then our most critical need is to find a viewpoint above the fray and distill clarity from all the complexity. We need some clearer head space in which we can collect our thoughts, reconnect with our raison d'être, reframe our perspective to better see the whole, and plot and lead a better way forward.

My own journey in this regard began long ago, as a young graduate. I recall attending my very first business conference—spending the first several hours stifling yawns as the succession of speakers delivered convoluted, slide-heavy, and jargon-laden presentations about their particular topics. They were data-rich but insight-poor (and essentially answer-free). Not only was I none the wiser at the end of each session, but I questioned how deeply the speakers really understood the problem themselves. A lot of words were used to say very little, or so it seemed to me. As former US Vice President Dan Quayle once said, without even a hint of irony, "verbosity leads to unclear, inarticulate things."

Then came the keynote speaker, a senior partner from one of the international strategy consultancies. He nailed it. The difference was like night and day. He demonstrated a truer grasp of the topic, not by regurgitating all the facts and figures, but by distilling for us the key insights that made the complex much clearer and more accessible. He wrapped his talk in a narrative that one could remember, convey to others, and act upon. It was clear, concise, and even elegant. The other speakers had painfully explained all the quandaries, whereas he revealed the simplicity hidden within, and the way through. In that moment, I said to myself, "Now, I want to be able to think like THAT!." It is a quest that continues to the present day, recognizing that, as Ernest Hemingway put it, "we are all apprentices in a craft where no one ever becomes a master."

Within a few years I moved to a larger city to take a job at a global consultancy. Feeling somewhat guilty about the hefty daily rates the firm was charging for me, I worked day and night to produce big, fat decks for my clients, hoping they might pass as good value for them. Chock-full of every framework and piece of analysis I could cram in. One day a partner took me aside and gave me some simple advice: "Never let methodology become a substitute for thinking," he said. I realized in that moment that I'd fallen into the same trap as those conference speakers. My clients weren't after a strategy report that made a deep thud as it hit the desk. What they really wanted was clarity. From that point on my reports gradually became more concise, the interactions more conversational, the insights sharper, the direction clearer, the language plainer, and the clients happier.

It has taken me years to appreciate the true power of purpose but one instance sowed a seed that later took root, becoming a tree of life.

I grew up on a wheat farm and was part of a small but tight-knit community where everybody looked out for each other, lending a hand whenever needed. The peak season is the harvest when all the farmers are out reaping their crops, the end-result of their year's investment and hard work. It is a hectic time when everyone works long hours to make sure the grain is taken off while the conditions are good. If not, all will be lost. So, everything else is put on hold until it's done. One year, at the beginning of harvest season, my beautiful mother, the very heart of our family, passed away. She was just forty-six. We were devastated and not in any state to go out to work, being unable to contemplate anything beyond our grief.

The day after her funeral I heard a dull roar outside the homestead. There in our wheatfields were all the neighboring farmers with their machinery. They had temporarily halted their own harvest at this most critical time of year to come and take care of ours. They didn't announce anything beforehand or make a big deal about it. They just came and did it. It was the most literal and practical case I'd seen of "loving your neighbor as yourself." Though it may be largely unspoken, in this rural community and others like it, farming families are clear on their purpose. It is not only to make a living but to make a life for themselves and their families. They intuitively know that succeeding depends on everyone considering the interests of their neighbors to be as important as their own. The social capital of their community is essential not only for the emotional connection it brings but as insurance on the day they need to make a call for help. Going back generations my family had made many deposits in that proverbial account. But on this day we were the ones who needed to draw on it. And we received help without even having to ask. To this day the image of that row of harvesters at work brings a tear to my eye and a sense of resolve. I would do likewise for those in need.

Over the years I've had many more such humbling experiences, too many to list here. They extend from the local to the global. The issues have ranged from child well-being to economic development and the contexts from apartheid-era South Africa to the slums of India to the headquarters of major companies and institutions. Each experience has only added to my resolve.

For me the most inspiring examples of purpose-driven leadership are not so much the well-worn corporate case studies or the billionaire entrepreneurs, as interesting as they are. Rather, it's the everyday heroes I've encountered in communities and social ventures around the world. I don't always remember their names, but their conviction, vitality, and leadership are not easily forgotten. What others may once have dismissed as idealism or even foolishness in taking on big challenges often turned out to be the very thing that demonstrated the true power of purpose in effecting change. "It always seems impossible until it's done," Nelson

Mandela said. And as with his story, a compelling purpose, a change that *must* be brought about, is at the core of every great transformation.

In my own career I've worked in both commercial companies and nonprofits. From start-ups to multinational corporations to global non-government organizations (NGOs). I've been responsible for annual revenues ranging from the tens of millions of dollars to billions of dollars. I've been a founder, chief marketing officer, chief strategy officer, chief innovation officer, chief executive officer, management consultant, board member, and even a professor for a time. Each of these varied experiences has added another dimension to my understanding of the relationship between cause and enterprise, purpose and profit. The consistent thread throughout those varied roles has been the search for strategic clarity in order to find a better way forward for all concerned—customers, staff, shareholders and society at large.

There is something in me that can't help but sidestep the orthodoxy of whatever environment I'm in, having something of a non-conformist streak. I'm always looking from different angles and asking the questions that others may not yet have posed. Not wanting to be rude or unduly disruptive, I invariably probe in a subtle and respectful manner. Sometimes the current way of thinking is indeed a reasonable one, and so after some explorations off to the side, I'll rejoin the conversation as it was originally framed. Often, however, a fresh perspective can be found that opens up a whole new world of possibility. I love that moment when the penny drops and someone says, "Aha! Why didn't we see that before?!"

We all need the aha moments of clarity that invariably precede a breakthrough. This is certainly true in the business world, but there are also plenty of nonprofits and other institutions who need to rediscover their raison d'être and way forward.

Purpose, strategy, and leadership are often thought of as "soft" factors. And yet they are amongst the most critical and hardest to master and convey. To refresh and reenergize our minds in this regard we need to be transported into a different headspace. Hence, I've tried to take a different approach with this book by stepping outside of conventional frames and case examples. Here you'll find little mention of what Fred Nerk, president of Acme, Inc., said, or what megapreneur Susan Scayle did, or a replication of what might typically be taught in an MBA course. There's only scant mention of Fortune 500 companies and nothing whatsoever about neuroscience, artificial intelligence, or the latest management theories. In any event, most of us don't work in the upper echelons of large corporations or have access to research teams or a busload of strategy consultants. In fact, many in purpose-driven organizations have much leaner circumstances to contend with. So, we'll focus on those competencies that tend to be more fundamental to success, universal in their application, and more enduring in their value.

My hope is that within these pages you will find cause to reimagine a better future for those you serve and for your organization—and a clearer path for getting there. If this book holds any ability to spark such thinking it will be more because it restores connection with powerful first principles. The intent here is to simplify key concepts, help disentangle the important from the incidental, and to clarify the strategic choices leaders should give greatest attention to.

By growing on purpose do we mean…

- growing on the basis of a compelling purpose?
- growing the enterprise with focused intent?
- growing revenues?
- growing impact?
- growing organizational capacity?

- growing in our corporate sense of meaning and possibility?
- growing in character and capability as leaders?

Yes! To all the above. Indeed, these are so intertwined as to be inseparable. For how can we sustainably grow income without also growing the meaning, value, and impact we have for those we serve? How can we expand our capacity without generating the funds to sustainably support that? How can we enhance the organization's sense of purpose without first growing ourselves as leaders? How can we do any of these things without having the kind of pioneering spirit, creativity and resilience that can only come from having a purpose worth pursuing?

This is growing on purpose for a purpose.

Herein are some of the key lessons I've picked up on my own journey thus far. I trust these will resonate with you, complement the lessons you've learned, and serve you well.

INTRODUCTION: THE CHALLENGE

Growing on Purpose

Power properly understood is nothing but the ability to achieve purpose. It is the strength required to bring about social, political, and economic change.... Now, we got to get this thing right. What is needed is a realization that power without love is reckless and abusive, and that love without power is sentimental and anemic. Power at its best is love implementing the demands of justice, and justice at its best is love correcting everything that stands against love. And this is what we must see as we move on...[1]

—DR. MARTIN LUTHER KING JR.

For the purposes of this book, we will substitute the word *growth* for "power" and *purpose* for "love" as described in Dr. King's message.

Growth is power in that it signals breakthrough, momentum, ascendancy. Growth has meaning not when it is pursued for its own sake, or is an end in and of itself, but rather when it is in the service of something greater. Growth indicates that we're making progress. That we're offering something of value to others. That we're learning. It brings about an increase not only in capital, but also capability and influence. It puts us in a position to achieve more.

With that comes responsibility.

Purpose is akin to love to the extent that it shifts our focus to something bigger than ourselves: from me to we and toward a greater good. It is a truer, more complete, more enduring, and more mutual form of value. It is the compelling reason why one would choose to step out from comfort, anonymity, or the safety of the crowd in order to go after the new, the better, the extraordinary. And for that matter, why others would be adventurous enough to join them.

Purpose provides the motivation and meaning. Growth is the means to see it progressively realized, day by day.

The kind of purpose being contemplated here has little to do with the platitudes we so often hear or the cliché statements that headline many annual reports but which hold little sway over key decisions during the year. Neither is it naiveté around the complexity of the challenges we face. It is not just this year's trending topic or management fad du jour. A truly purpose-driven endeavor will be inspired not only by a vision of the way things could be, but most likely by some level of alarm at the current state and a sober acceptance of the call to effect change. As Dr. King also went on to say, *"I'm not talking about emotional bosh when I talk about love; I'm talking about a strong, demanding love. For I have seen too much hate…. The road ahead will not always be smooth…. There will be inevitable setbacks here and there…. [But] difficult and painful as it is, we must walk on in the days ahead with an audacious faith in the future."*[2]

This is the kind of purpose in which we are ready to share in both the prize and the price.

The evidence of a deep dissatisfaction with the status quo—the continued dissonance between growth and purpose, between the promise and the experience—is all around us. Trust in institutions has been in long-term decline, not only with governments and banks but the nonprofit sector as well. Only one in five people believe that the system as it stands is working for them. More than 70 percent report a sense of injustice, perceiving the society's elites are using the system to their advantage and to the detriment of others. They want to see purpose-driven reformers and innovators in those positions of power, bringing about the changes that are needed.[3]

Almost 80 percent of business leaders believe that purpose is central to organizational success and yet only around one-third say they meaningfully factor that into their decision-making processes.[4] Almost three-quarters of employees believe that their companies could take actions that would both increase profits and improve economic and social prosperity. And yet, based on their actual experience, 85 percent say they do not feel engaged.[5]

Globally, the clear majority of consumers prefer to buy from companies that act responsibly and stand for a purpose that resonates with them, even if that means paying more.[6] Brands that consumers see as serving a worthy and meaningful purpose have grown at more than twice the rate of others.[7]

Consumers assess more than just the message of cause-related marketing campaigns. They also watch the wider behavior set of the company and its leadership. They've developed a finely tuned radar for PR spin, doublespeak, and "good washing." Many understand the power they have to influence company direction, through their purchasing behaviors, feedback, and social influence. More than ever before they will walk away from organizations that do not have a relevant purpose, or don't live up to their promises.

In such an environment the only way to grow sustainably is through a deeper and more authentic pursuit of a purpose that matters to both you and your stakeholders. Not just because it is the right thing to do, but because it informs us how to do things right. A shared purpose invites others to co-create with us. With that comes the opportunity to innovate and to learn from mistakes without breaking trust.

In the philanthropic sphere we see more donors thinking like growth-minded investors, wanting to see their contributions do double duty: growing both social impact and organizational sustainability. Hence the rise of more scalable self-sustaining models such as microfinance, impact investment, and social enterprise.

Consider the case of BRAC, a Bangladeshi nonprofit that is now the world's largest community development NGO, reaching more than 126 million people annually. Around three-quarters of its work is self-funded through the proceeds of its own social enterprises and investments—which span agriculture, fisheries, education, renewable energy, paper, printing, banking, insurance, and technology. These serve to simultaneously address unmet needs, create channels to market for the poor, provide fair prices for farmers, and generate employment opportunities. The financial surpluses from these social enterprises are reinvested into innovation and community initiatives, thereby increasing development effectiveness and reducing reliance on foreign donors. An astonishing achievement when one considers the highly resource-constrained regions in which BRAC operates.[8]

Whatever sector one is coming from, there is a clear need and opportunity for leaders who understand what it takes to grow on the basis of, and for the ends of, a worthy and compelling purpose.

Growth for its own sake, outside of purpose, is hollow and therefore unsustainable. Purpose without growth has limited impact. The two are meant to work in concert, not in competition. In right combination they have the power to create both economic and social prosperity, restoring to fuller potential that which may have been overlooked, kept down, underserved, broken, or unfairly held back.

To sow in this manner is to participate in a greater harvest. To be on the right side of history. It is to boldly step forward to overcome challenges rather than timidly holding back and eventually being overtaken or made irrelevant. Our world (our markets, customers, staff, society, environment) is groaning because the old mindsets and models are insufficient, and in some cases serve to perpetuate the problem.

The gaps left by others present both the need and the opportunity for leaders who are more genuinely purpose-driven to step forward and find a better way. Now is the time to rethink the way forward. To grow on purpose.

- Our need as a **world** is to see these kinds of shifts en masse.
- Our need as **organizations** is to find our full and proper place within this bigger picture, playing a role that is both life giving and value creating.
- Our need as **leaders** is to find the place of strategic clarity from which we can see and articulate our organization's purpose and map out how we will grow in that, such that others will want to be part of the journey.
- Our need as **individuals** is for meaning. Purpose transforms our work, and that of our staff, into a vocation—perhaps even something that might be regarded a calling.

The Underlying Problem

"Pressure is what you feel when you don't know what's going on."
—Chuck Noll

Every well-intentioned leader sets out to take their organization forward in a way that accelerates progress. They believe it is genuinely possible. Stakeholders welcome the fresh views and energy that a new leader brings. It's champagne, media releases, hundred-day plans, and hockey stick projections all round. (And, no doubt, a restructure going on quietly in the background). We've all seen it. We ourselves may have been that leader.

Fast-forward a year later and clichéd expressions such as "it's like walking through molasses" may well start to resonate. Headwinds may have developed into a perfect storm. As a result, the proverbial ducks are neither flying in formation nor standing in a row. The internal silos seem to be rebuilding themselves even after we thought they'd been dismantled. The parking lot of issues to be addressed is jammed. Our plate is full and we're drinking from a fire hose. The elephant is still in the room, and the eight hundred-pound gorilla is lurking nearby. Even after peeling the onion the answers are still not entirely clear. The board chairperson starts a conversation with "I know you've been working hard, *but…*," echoing the signals we might also have been receiving from the family at home who've seen us become increasingly stressed and unavailable. Despite earlier high hopes we now begin to manage expectations.

No one promised it'd be easy, and anyone in a leadership role is going to be busy. Nevertheless, the pressure rises when we feel unsure of what's going on and hence begin to lose control of the strategic agenda. This may be either because of a fog of uncertainties or a fray of competing demands. Or, most likely, a combination of both.

"The fog of war" is an apt metaphor as it conflates both the uncertainty (i.e., the fog) and difficulty of perception and decision-making in a tumultuous and competitive operating environment (i.e., the fray). This may be equally true for both those leaders at headquarters and those on the frontline. It was made famous by former US secretary of state Robert S. McNamara in reference to the Vietnam War (and later used as the title of the 2004 documentary of his life). The original thought is attributed to the Prussian general and military theorist von Clausewitz who said, "War is the realm of uncertainty; three quarters of the factors on which action in war is based are wrapped in a fog of greater or lesser uncertainty. A sensitive and discriminating judgment is called for; a skilled intelligence to scent out the truth." Substitute the word *war* for the particular mission you've embarked upon, and that advice may well ring true.

So how do we contend with our own strategic fog?

Of course, the specific challenges we face will be unique to our own contexts. However, when it comes to seeking strategic clarity there are four patterns at play that will tend to limit our thinking. Understanding the nature of these restraining forces is key to breaking free of them. They are: complexity; convention; constraint; and conflict.

complexity

*"There is a point of complexity beyond which a business
is no longer manageable."*

—Peter Drucker

Leading an organization is becoming an increasingly complex undertaking. We're seeing rapid and often disruptive shifts in the economic, social, political, regulatory, and technological environments in which we must operate, A majority of senior decision-makers recognize it as a significant challenge for them personally, and for their organization—around 70 percent, in fact, according to KPMG.[9] It's no wonder that one major study found that CEOs spend almost twice as much time with consultants as they do with their own customers.[10]

We've a dilemma. On the one hand the complexity is real and must be dealt with. We can't just ignore it. On the other, it's hard to be decisive when the answer to every question seems to begin with the words, "well, it depends." Somehow the issues have to be distilled without being diluted.

An organization captured by complexity is likely to experience symptoms such as slow or cautious decision-making, mixed messages, siloing, inefficient processes, and staff uncertainty—none of which we can afford if we are to continue growing on purpose.

The reasons for the rise in complexity are many and varied. For now, suffice it to say that these can be considered in two broad categories:

1. **External**: those that come with the territory we're in, and over which we may have limited influence. The difficulty or ambiguity may arise from policy uncertainty, the effects of new laws or technology, market forces, the speed of innovation in the sector,

new entrants, shifting stakeholder expectations, or a wide range of other pressures.

2. **Internal**: those we inflict on ourselves. Complexity should be embraced to the extent necessary to properly understand the issues and options before us. The problem is more one of unnecessary complication: adding more and more organizational functions, policies, programs, meetings, applications, data, frameworks, tools, risk assessments, decision steps. Often these are reactive measures that don't easily integrate with each other or consider their knock-on effect (which is usually added complication for others in the organization). As with any system there's a point at which all the modifications, extra rules, and add-ons start to slow the whole system down, or even cause it to crash. As with any organ transplant, the organizational antibodies may fight against the new, no matter how essential to survival it may be.

Our challenge is made even more difficult by the increasing competition and accelerating pace of change most of us contend with. The world won't pause long enough for us to find our bearings or press the reset button. And it won't become any less dynamic or convoluted in future.

convention

"Why fit in when you were born to stand out?"

—Dr. Seuss

Conventions in themselves are not necessarily a problem. They can bring civility, order and collaboration to a field that might otherwise be chaotic. We may adhere to conventions because that's the way things are done in a particular industry, market, or organizational culture—and we see no reason to rock the boat. There's often a sense of safety and responsibility in doing things the same way as others in our space. That's a fine thing when it comes to interoperability, professional ethics, or quality standards. But in any endeavor where *difference* is key to creating value, conventions could have the effect of eroding our advantage. It becomes especially perilous when we adopt groupthink without even realizing that we've done so (which is to say, we've been captured by conventional wisdom). This may be introduced inadvertently through actions such as:

- following industry best practices,
- emulating competitors,
- incremental budgeting,
- outsourcing core business functions to a shared service provider,
- using others' case studies as our primary source of learning,
- engaging consultants that have done similar work for others,
- securing contracts through highly specified open requests for tender,
- participating in a third-party platform where others define the rules, and
- subscribing to the same market research studies or going to the same conferences.

Though there may be a perfectly reasonable prima facie case for actions such as these, there may also be unintended consequences. To some extent each of the above actions may have the effect of:

- dulling ambition, especially if current best practices limit our aspiration and cause us to behave more like imitators than true innovators;
- allowing someone else's frame or rules to define the issues and supersede our own unique views and alternative ideas; or
- causing competitors' business practices to become more like each other (i.e., pushing enterprises toward the mean for their sector, or otherwise reducing options or differentiation).

Therein lies the key difference between leaders and followers. Between those building for the future and those oriented toward short-term fixes.

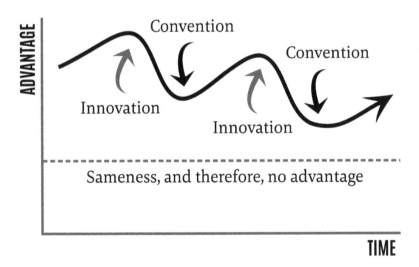

We cannot cut our way to growth or imitate our way to breakthrough. Yet so many organizations have effectively slipped into this way of thinking. It's no wonder many customers find it hard to choose between providers. They all look the same. And it's no wonder that many sectors are being disrupted by those willing to play differently.

The logic underpinning many such actions can be thought of as reasoning by analogy. In effect, something is considered to be a good idea because leading Entrepreneur A, Company B, or Government C is doing it. "It worked for them. It seems to make sense to us, and we can shorten our learning curve if we adopt their way of thinking." Many times such a decision may be perfectly valid. But here's the thing: you don't really know if that's your best option unless you've done some original thinking of your own. Until you have stripped away conventional practices and assumptions, taken the problem back to first principles, and reconceived other alternative ways forward, you won't know what works best. Reasoning by analogy is essentially a mental shortcut. Original thinking can produce deeper understanding, fresh perspectives, and new options, which is especially important for our bigger strategic decisions. It is the difference between the cook who follows a recipe and the chef who creates an inspired new dish.

This is not to say that we need to rethink everything, or that there isn't a place for conventions and analogy. It's just that leaders ought to think through the full implications of their choices and be clear about what they may be trading off. Sometimes we do need to learn from others or accept certain rules. Sometimes we need to save time and effort in one area in order to invest in another. There's value in understanding the current state of best practice as a baseline, so we can make explicit choices about where we'll meet it, how we can beat it, or even when to retreat from that space altogether in order to play elsewhere.

To constantly innovate is not without its risks, and so one ought to think carefully about where and how to push forward in this regard. But then again, there are few circumstances in which one should settle for being merely average. Most value tends to be captured by the top two or three enterprises in an industry. Most customers prefer to deal with leading providers. The best talent gravitates toward companies with a compelling purpose and who are breaking new ground. Therefore, as leaders we should be careful about making choices that may cause the organization to descend toward the middle of the pack. It's important to be aware of what others are doing, but not merely settle for that ourselves. As with rules, best practices are meant to be broken, either by exceeding them or rewriting the standard altogether. This is especially true when it comes to the key factors that underpin our competitive edge, whether that's quality, cost, scale, speed, reach, experience, capabilities, culture, or other such advantage. Even if we're in an ostensibly non-competitive sphere, such as government, why only aspire to a benchmark set by somebody else when the world is constantly changing, when our own context may need a different answer, when we could lead, and when continued innovation could deliver ever-better value to all our stakeholders?

Author and organizational leader Warren Bennis put it this way: "People who cannot invent and reinvent themselves must be content with borrowed postures, second-hand ideas, fitting in instead of standing out."

constraint

> *"Give me a lever long enough and a place to stand,*
> *and I shall move the world."*
>
> —Archimedes

The central economic problem is said to be the question of how we allocate our limited resources to satisfy seemingly unlimited needs. That applies at both the micro level (the enterprise) and the macro level (the economy). A start-up venture trying to get off the ground. A nonprofit trying to meet the social needs around them. Or a secretary of the treasury or finance minister trying to prioritize the various projects and services a government wants to deliver. This certainly relates to money, which is the resource that's generally at the top of everyone's mind. But there are other valuable resources to be considered, not the least of which is our time and talent. In many cases these are even more scarce and more critical to success.

We will inevitably have to say no to some activities in order to invest in others. We will have to choose what gets addressed and what doesn't. Or sometimes we may settle for a compromise solution. C'est la vie. Determining what we *won't do* is just as important as deciding what we *will*.

Scarcity arises not only from the resource side of the equation (e.g., what is or isn't in our bank account) but also from our ambition. The imbalance between the two is the issue. The more substantial the aspiration, the harder it is to lift. Some address this by lightening their goals, setting their sights lower. For a genuinely purpose-driven organization, seeking to achieve something greater than itself, this may not be an option. It may have to find some other way to tip the scales.

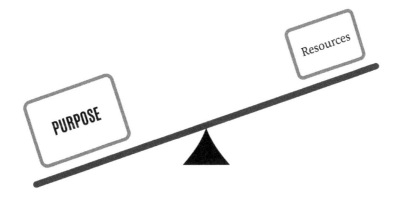

Decisions about where to allocate our limited resources are rarely purely objective or dispassionate, even if analysts or academics sometimes frame choices in this way. In practice these can be gut-wrenching decisions and their implications profound. Real lives and livelihoods are being affected. That can weigh heavily on us.

I recall a difficult visit to an urban slum in India. At the time I was with an international development NGO working in that community. A woman approached me unexpectedly. She was begging with me, through an interpreter, to allow her daughter to stay in school. (The daughter had just reached the age threshold after which the program funding cut out). The mother was down on her knees, kissing my hand, crying, and pleading. She was just as concerned for her child as I would have been about my own, had our roles been reversed. Such education is key to finding one's way out of poverty. I felt awful. I so wanted to say yes, but I didn't have the authority to do so, and our organization didn't have the resources to extend the program any further. In that moment I considered paying for her daughter's schooling out of my own pocket, but then how could I cherry-pick one family in that way?

How would my Indian colleagues implement this one-off case? How would that exception be explained to the rest of that community or the million equally deserving people our NGO was working with in India? My encounter with the mother was only for a few minutes, but I still feel that knot in my stomach years later. The true nature of poverty is not just the absence of money, but more profoundly it is the lack of freedom in determining one's own future. I desperately wanted to find a way around our own constraints to help her, and the many other families in the same situation, but I just didn't know how.

When seen through the eyes of the people affected, this challenge of limited resources in the face of unlimited needs is not nearly so abstract or dry as the economic language we often employ. Not everyone will experience circumstances as dire as this mother and daughter. By comparison most of us have so-called first-world problems, such as finding the right school for our child. Nevertheless, scarcity is real and comes in all forms. We have a purpose worth pursuing, an important need that must be met, but we don't possess everything we need to bring that about. Nevertheless, there are some people who do manage to punch well above their weight. There are leaders, policymakers, innovators, entrepreneurs, activists, and other change agents who have managed to achieve a lot with relatively little. Such people tend not to compromise on their sense of purpose. Instead, they use what they do have in more insightful, targeted, and creative ways. In one form or another they are seeking leverage. This may be through combining their resources with others, finding a longer lever (thereby amplifying the force of the resources they do have) and/or finding a strategic position (fulcrum) closer to the real opportunity on which to turn the game to their advantage. By thinking differently, they increase their options or power, breaking out of at least some of the constraints that might otherwise have held them back.

We can't change the nature of economics. We may not be able to change our situation. But could it be that sometimes it is really our thinking that is constrained? If those with an entrepreneurial mindset can find a way forward in challenging circumstances, maybe we could too? Sometimes the brick wall we hit is what it is, and there's no way around it. But then how will we know until we've explored all the angles or levers available to us?

conflict

*"A business that makes nothing but money is a
poor kind of business."*

—Henry Ford

In any organization there will be differing viewpoints and schools of thought. Such diversity is a natural part of business and indeed can be a wellspring of insight, creativity, and energy when these perspectives come together within a healthy culture. But there's one debate that continues to sit rather awkwardly in many organizations. That is the relationship between purpose and profit (or financial sustainability in the case of nonprofits).

Purpose and profit are so fundamental to an enterprise that if the relationship between them is conflicted it will eventually trip them up. A house divided against itself in this way will have difficulty standing tall, or perhaps, at all. Such a company would ultimately risk failure through either irrelevancy or insolvency (either one of which leads to the other anyway).

Purpose and profit ought to be the most synergistic of partnerships. Conceptually they complement one another perfectly. Purpose is our very reason for being. It is the foundational idea that informs what we do, where we play, who we serve, what we prioritize, why others would join us. Profit comes as a result of doing that well. Simple, isn't it? And yet purpose and profit are often spoken about as though they are trade-offs.

Even with best intentions the stated purpose of many companies ends up being somewhat compromised when, in effect, they're largely bolting social responsibility programs onto a business model that's fully geared for the profit motive. Profit is seen as real, substantial, quantifiable, and therefore numero uno. Purpose is perhaps seen as soft, idealistic, indirect, and therefore more of a nice-to-have commodity. There may be sincere efforts to be socially responsible, but actually realizing a higher purpose is usually some way off.

Conversely, the thought of becoming more financially self-sustaining appeals to many benevolent organizations. In practice, however, it is a struggle to do what that takes in practice. Therefore, many continue in their dependence on donors or taxpayers, unable to invest in growth unless someone else grants part of *their profits* toward the cause.

It is somewhat of a curiosity that we categorize some of our most important organizations by what they're *not: not*-for-profits (NFPs) or *non*-government organizations (NGOs). Surely there's a more important frame with which to identify them—such as the purpose for which they stand (i.e., what it is that they are here *for*, their mission). Similarly, we call commercial companies *for*-profit, but again surely profit is the by-product of a higher purpose or mission.

This goes to the question of which sits on the throne in our thinking: purpose or profit? They ultimately need each other. Ideally, they should complement one another within the same business model. But they can't both be sovereign. Occasionally there will be times when their interests can't be served equally, when one must bow to the other. Is profit the greater goal, or is a company's purpose or mission the most important thing? Does profit serve purpose? Or is purpose ultimately only a tool with which to generate profit?

The quandary we experience today arises out of views like that of economist Milton Friedman who famously said, "there is one and only one social responsibility of business—to use its resources and engage in activities designed to increase its profits."[11] In this worldview the leaders of a company are employed by the shareholders, and it is their interests that are preeminent. They provide the capital with an expectation of a return (i.e., shareholder value). Therefore, the primary *purpose* of a company is *profit*. The two have become conflated. Even if the organization did start out with a great purpose, you might say that capital staged a coup and took over the kingdom.

This conflict sits within a capitalist paradigm from which much good has come. We have seen huge leaps in global wealth creation and poverty alleviation as a result of capitalism. It's the best system we have at present, but that is not to say it's without some serious flaws. Because it is designed around profit making, it doesn't deal well with important needs from which there is no potential to profit. These needs have to be met by redistributive activities like taxes and philanthropy. Those with money (e.g., investors) have the advantage of being able to make more, and the wealth created at this top doesn't always trickle down to the less advantaged. Some will influence government policy or company decisions in a way that prefers their own interests over those of other key stakeholders, such as customers, staff, and society in general. As a result, inequality widens.

The system persists because it's the only viable one we have today. Nevertheless, it is groaning; power is shifting. Citizens are better informed and are using their voice more forcefully. Consumers have a finely tuned radar for providers that don't live up to their values or promises. Staff seek more than just a paycheck. Many shareholders are more concerned about ethics and sustainability than ever before. One gets the sense that the preconditions of a paradigm shift are in place—perhaps one in which purpose and profit can regain more of the symbiotic relationship they always should have enjoyed.

In any event, to equivocate on this most fundamental issue of profit and purpose is to be double minded on the most pivotal questions of strategy. We have to be clear in our decision-making. Our staff, customers, and stakeholders want clarity, conviction, and consistency. And yet we often struggle to get it right.

*"The greatest danger for most of us is not that our aim is too high
and we miss it, but that it is too low and we reach it."*

—Michelangelo

Complexity. Convention. Constraint. Conflict. Each of these forces nudge us toward a narrower frame at a time when we need to think bigger. They push us toward unsatisfying compromises, a lowering of ambition, a dulling of creativity.

It's human nature to gravitate to the known and the more tangible even if there's the potential for a better result in another, less familiar space. Even when we intuitively know we need to pursue new options, we still tend to slip back toward incrementalism in an attempt to minimize risk. This apparent safety may be illusionary however, especially when the environment is changing rapidly and others are willing to break out of the box.

The problem is exacerbated when we're under time pressure. We're busy. Perhaps we have an upcoming board meeting at which we're due to present a strategy, so we might compromise by utilizing the most familiar or practical options we have at hand. In effect the tactical becomes a substitute for the strategic:

- plans substitute for strategy
- methodology substitutes for our own thinking
- data substitutes for insight
- someone else's frame substitutes for our own
- imitation substitutes for imagination
- incrementalism substitutes for innovation
- reorganizing substitutes for genuine transformation
- a series of short-term results substitute for a sustainable growth path

- activity substitutes for progress
- charity substitutes for justice
- management substitutes for leadership
- caution substitutes for courage
- profit substitutes for purpose.

All of the former options above are important. We clearly need plans, analysis, short-term wins, and the like. We certainly need good management. We need charity. But if we want to really lead, these things must be complements to, and not substitutes for, the latter.

So, what is the way forward? What do we need to do as leaders if we are to break out of the box? To start with, excellence in three key areas: consistency of purpose, strategic clarity, and leadership agility. These are often recognized but rarely mastered in practice. The hope of this book is to help you more fully apprehend these, and thereby, grow on purpose. Strengthening any one of these will serve you well, but when all three are working in unison, new realms of opportunity become available.

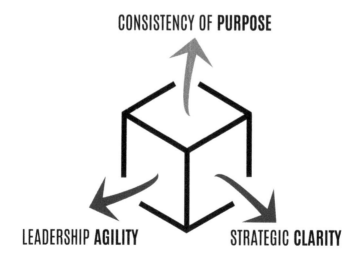

Consistency of purpose is about a centered and sustained commitment to an important cause. Such dedication is a necessary basis for any real advancement over time. Look beneath the surface of just about any endeavor that has had lasting impact (and the growth that often accompanies that), and you'll find genuine commitment to an end-goal worthy of the pursuit. Even many of the apparent overnight successes we see are really founder or advocate journeys over many years prior. They may have had to tack into the wind on many occasions, but they rarely wavered from the purpose that compelled them to set off from the shore. Not only have they been consistent in the pursuit of this purpose *across time* but also *across activities*. Everything is designed to be part of a cohesive whole, working toward the same ultimate end—from culture to products, from brand to systems, from the receptionist to the CEO. Even across the diversity of functions and people, there is a certain intentionality, harmony, and flow. Their original vision may have ended up taking some surprising twists and turns, but even so they kept the faith and stayed true. Such deep commitment to purpose is not just hanging onto what might seem like a quaint ideal. Rather it is an understanding of the breakthrough power that can be found in focus, integrity, persistence, and authentic care for those we serve.

Strategic clarity is the product of strategic thinking, the seeking of a higher and more holistic perspective. It is not easy or quick, but it is possible to ascend that hill in order to gain a better appreciation of the landscape and the opportunities beyond. The view is well worth the climb. Generally, we don't mind putting in the hard work, or investing, or taking calculated risks. But not knowing what to make of our environment or what course to chart, can be debilitating. In those times we crave simplicity. Just knowing the right *direction* to head in would be enough, even if we can't foresee every challenge that we may encounter along the way. Such lucidity rarely comes at once and so we must embark on a journey of exploration, discernment, and discovery, allowing some aspects to unfold over time.

Leadership agility allows for adaptation in a tactical sense whilst also remaining true to our longer-term strategy and intent. Being agile is not a virtue in itself, for that would mean constantly dodging, weaving, and pivoting without a clear understanding of the destination—an exhausting prospect. But, when agility is combined with the stability and meaning provided by purpose, and the bigger picture clarity that comes from strategic thinking, it can become a means of making unexpected, and perhaps even accelerated progress toward your true goal. "Chance favors the prepared mind."[12] Some forces can be foreseen and factored into one's plans, but the reality is that there are still many challenges that we must contend with as they arise. A disruptive change in regulation. The entry of a new competitor. The unexpected loss of a major customer or funding source or key employee. A cyberattack. A pandemic. If we're willing to lead with agility, such roadblocks can be overcome, or even be used for good.

These three dimensions complement one another perfectly, together creating the head space with which we might see and pursue greater opportunities for both impact and growth. And, like the small rudder on a large ship, they have a profound effect on our setting, destination, and ability to navigate the seas in between.

PART I

CONSISTENCY OF PURPOSE

"The secret of success is constancy to purpose."

—BENJAMIN DISRAELI

The basis of success for any genuinely purpose-driven organization is contained in the term itself: a *purpose* that goes after a compelling need worthy of our highest and best endeavors. And secondly, *consistency* (or *drivenness* if you will) in our pursuit of that. Therein is the focus and persistence needed to break through. The extent to which we have been true in both these regards is the extent to which we can authentically claim the title and anticipate meaningful progress.

ONE

UNDERSTANDING PURPOSE

"There is no failure except failure to serve one's purpose."

—HENRY FORD

I
f we are to tap into the true power of purpose, we must first comprehend it at a deeper level than the somewhat glib manner in which it is often used. Properly understood, purpose is the single most fundamental driver of both impact and growth. It is the lens through which we find strategic clarity. It is the very essence of good leadership. Purpose is the on-ramp we choose because of the destination we have in mind. It is the moral compass that orients the journey thereafter. Purpose helps us define important milestones along the way. Quite simply, there is no more important consideration to be clear on first, either in this book or in your own efforts to make a difference.

Let us examine purpose from three complementary perspectives:

1. Purpose as motive.
2. Purpose as a platform.
3. Purpose as a catalyst.

Purpose as Motive

You may be familiar with the phrase *motive, means and opportunity* from watching crime shows on television. They are the three key elements the prosecutor needs to persuade the jury of their case and thereby gain a conviction. In reality it's a little more complicated than that, but nevertheless it helps frame the story of the investigation. We might also use this as a metaphor for organizational purpose, with a slight play on those words. That is, purpose as motive, *meaning* and opportunity.

The Oxford Dictionary defines purpose as, "the reason for which something is done or created or for which something exists." In this we find both *motive* (why we're on this journey, what drives us) and *meaning* (why that matters). Purpose can also be defined as "a sense of resolve or determination", or to "have as one's intention or objective." [1]In this we see an act of pressing forward toward some future *opportunity* or possibility.

An organization's purpose is its collective "why," its raison d'être, its most important reason for being. In practice, however, expressions of an organization's purpose tend to take on one of two very different flavors: bland or rich.

The bland view of purpose is functionally based, almost as though the enterprise were little more than an espresso machine, the purpose of which is to "make coffee." The bland purpose or mission statements of many organizations reflect a similarly dry view, offering such generic aims as "delivering quality service," "satisfying customers," "leading the market," and "generating profit." Such goals may be entirely appropriate, but they're not particularly distinctive, instructive, or inspiring. Nor do they suggest anything of a deeper motivation or higher aspiration. They are focused on the What not the Why. This very limited view of purpose pulls them toward conventional thinking, short-sightedness and sameness—the very things we wish to avoid. The richer kind of purpose is of a different complexion.

In order for a purpose to come to life it has to give life, being imbued with meaning for the community of stakeholders being served. The richest purposes are those that lift our sights. They tap into our need to serve something greater. They possess an air of inevitability, and the power of an idea whose time has come. As Martin Luther King Jr. said, "the arc of the moral universe is long, but it bends toward justice." The subtext in this, as in many great expressions of purpose, is essentially, "this is big, but it's necessary and right. Though it may be difficult, we will innovate and persist until we prevail. You have a part to play. Please join us."

True purpose is not a product to sell or a program to deliver. Rather, it is a deeply important need to be met, a critical problem to be solved, a vastly better future to unlock. It upholds that which we most value and the end we ultimately seek. And, if we're on board, it should also resonate with us at a more individual level, answering the question: Why am I committing myself to this cause and this organization as a leader, employee, customer, investor, donor, volunteer, advocate, business partner or in any other such capacity?

This question of "why does our organization exist?" is surely the most fundamental, and yet the most skimmed-over question in business. We spend the vast majority of our time debating and planning the What, How, Where, and When. And yet, the answer to this higher-order question of Why profoundly affects everything that follows. It defines the basis of success. It reminds us why we put ourselves on the line every day. Why it's worth innovating and investing and taking calculated risks. Why others should consider joining or aligning with us.

To be clear on our why—our purpose—is to shed light on all the other questions crying out for a better answer. Moreover, it helps tie all those choices together into a cohesive whole. If we know why we're here and why something is important, it helps clarify where we need to be playing, who we should be working with, and what kinds of activities we might need to engage in. And if it's a worthy purpose greater than ourselves, it will attract the attention of others whose support we'll need if we are to succeed.

Far from being neglected, our purpose ought to be our first and last reflection at work each and every day. It ought to frame every pivotal decision we make.

Indeed, *if we're not serving a deeply compelling and worthwhile purpose, then what on earth are we doing?* Life is short. Time is precious. Talent and resources are scarce. Why would we want to expend those things on furiously spinning a hamster wheel that produces little of enduring value?

Sometimes we read articles or hear speakers framing purpose as a relatively new development. A trend. The latest management method with which to drive performance. Or something that has recently come to the fore because of a greater social consciousness amongst employees, investors, and consumers. But to conceive of purpose only as a matter of vogue, or as an external market shift requiring a response, is to have missed the point. Such framing suggests that the author may themselves have only recently realized the importance of that which was always fundamental. For at what time prior to the so-called trend was it ever a good idea to start, lead or grow an enterprise without having a clear reason for being? And when was it ever a good idea to invest our time, talents, and resources in an endeavor that produces no social good or has no lasting positive effect?

The fact is that purpose has always been foundational. We've varied only in how much attention we've paid it, and the degree to which we've been true in its execution. The extent to which one understands, values, and participates in the organization's purpose will largely determine both how motivated and creative they are—and the level of meaning they derive from that endeavor.

People are wired to seek meaning in their personal and corporate lives. We need to know that what we're signing up for is of genuine benefit. That we're participating in something that really matters. We tend not to engage fully, releasing the best we have to give, unless we first find meaning in the challenge before us.

Purpose imbues meaning and motivation by helping us

- locate ourselves within something greater
- find reason for hope, and to look for the good that we can do
- understand why the endeavor deserves our very best
- give expression to what we stand for
- frame and interpret what is happening around us
- see connections we might not otherwise have made
- rise above the busyness, transcend chaos, see events in context
- discern the important from the urgent
- guide our collective efforts toward creating a better future
- enjoy more aligned relationships with like-minded colleagues
- have our contribution recognized, and valued, by others.

A great purpose is one that is pregnant with possibility. It is bold and stretching, and yet tantalizingly feasible. Somehow it calls to us, challenging us to step into that picture, into the gap between what is and what could be. Consider the difference between these reported examples of purpose statements:

"To organize the world's information and make it universally accessible and useful." (Google)

"Spread ideas." (TED)

"To provide a free, world-class education for anyone, anywhere." (Khan Academy)

"To help create lasting solutions to the injustice of poverty." (Oxfam)

"To accelerate the world's transition to sustainable energy." (Tesla)

"To conserve the land and waters on which all life depends." (The Nature Conservancy)

"To help people around the world plan and have the perfect trip." (TripAdvisor)

"To create shareholder and societal value while reducing the environmental footprint along the value chains in which we operate." (DuPont)

"To collect, preserve, study, exhibit, and stimulate appreciation for and advance knowledge of works of art that collectively represent the broadest spectrum of human achievement at the highest level of quality, all in the service of the public and in accordance with the highest professional standards." (MoMA)

"Real food that matters for life's moments." (Campbell Soups)

"To fill the world with emotion, through the power of creativity." (Sony)

The organizations listed here are all highly accomplished in their own way. But as you read these purpose or mission statements, which column inspires you more? The left, or right? Which focusses on the greater good? Which are more about the company's products than the need being addressed? Which seem more authentic, and conversely which seem more contrived? Which seem more like true change-makers? Which are more likely to attract top talent or new collaborators? Which make you want to scream, "Who cares?!" Which would hold more meaning and motivation for you as a leader? In which do you see greater opportunity?

Though those purpose statements in the left column may sound more idealistic, they beg the question, Why aim for less? On closer inspection we see that although these are big aspirations, they are also quite focused in terms of the problem to be solved. This places these purposes within the realm of the conceivable, rather than the grandiose. Though each is unlikely to be fully realized anytime soon, all progress toward these ends is entirely worthwhile, producing considerable good along the way.

Each of these organization's purposes are legitimate, for they are being genuinely pursued. These ideals pervade their cultures. Each organization's competencies and investments are aligned with that quest. Their money is placed where their mouth is, so to speak. Indeed, many have considerable momentum in this regard. The energy therein is compelling.

In my first role as a consultant, I joined an e-commerce start-up way back in the days when I still had hair and the World Wide Web was relatively new. Our clients were typically senior executives of large corporations. If you can imagine, this was a time when many still needed convincing that the Internet was going to radically transform their sectors. In some cases, leaders had already bought into that idea but needed help in determining how best to seize the growth opportunities this presented.

Ours was one of the first advisory firms to combine the disciplines of a strategy consultancy, a marketing agency, and a technology firm—something which is common today, but novel back then. We had an informal purpose statement of sorts, one which was only used internally. We aspired to be "the McKinsey of the Internet." No doubt we were flattering ourselves with the comparison. Nevertheless, it proved to be instructive and catalytic. It clearly implied that our role was to bring strategic clarity to large organizations, helping them use the Internet to transform their business models. Moreover, it informed how we positioned ourselves, where we played, who we'd work for, who we hired, how we dressed, how we charged, and the like. It was a simple, five-word aspiration, but one which helped us to grow rapidly and have considerable impact along the way. It may not rise to the standard of a true purpose statement as I would define it today, but it served as a prototype thereof, and was effective in providing us with motive, meaning, and opportunity.

Purpose as a Platform

An organization stripped bare of the artifacts that give it an identity (such as its legal incorporation, brand, storefronts, and the like) is essentially a group of people coming together for a purpose. Purpose is the platform on which the whole enterprise stands and the basis on which individuals combine their insights, talents, and efforts in pursuit of some greater good.

This is the case for any form of organization: business or nonprofit, school or university, church or community group, start-up venture or corporation, or government agency or multilateral institution. People come together in these various formations because there is a collective or societal need requiring collaborative effort. The undertaking is too great for any one person to achieve by themselves. An organization's purpose therefore spans the gap between those bigger needs and what individuals can achieve by themselves. It unites the latter to serve the former.

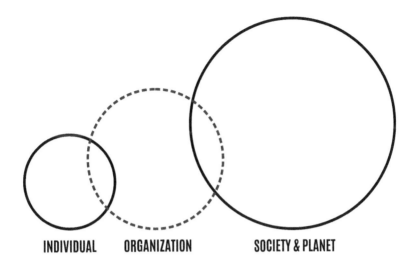

INDIVIDUAL   ORGANIZATION   SOCIETY & PLANET

The underlying questions for the individual in this picture might be Who am I? and Where might I best contribute to the greater good? The space in between the individual and society presents the possibility of shared purpose amongst like-minded people seeking similar ends. This is the domain of organizational (or corporate or collective or shared) purpose.

The personal sense of purpose of founders and any co-founders of an organization will drive the mission of their start up. If you're joining an established organization, it's important to consider its mission and ask yourself if your values can align with that. By opting into that corporate purpose, you are effectively aligning yourself to something bigger. You need to decide whether or not you are prepared to respect and adopt that purpose as part of your own.

Multiply that by a hundred if you're a leader in the organization. If you are to be its champion and role-model, you need to own that purpose authentically. It would be a disservice to yourself, to staff, to customers, and to all stakeholders if you aren't all in with the mission.

Let's dig a little deeper into this idea of purpose as a platform. There are three levels to an organization's purpose.

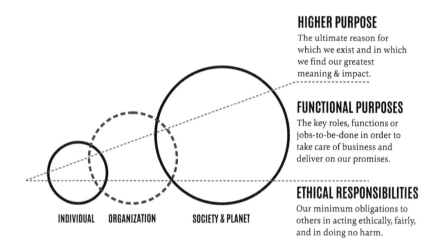

HIGHER PURPOSE
The ultimate reason for which we exist and in which we find our greatest meaning & impact.

FUNCTIONAL PURPOSES
The key roles, functions or jobs-to-be-done in order to take care of business and deliver on our promises.

ETHICAL RESPONSIBILITIES
Our minimum obligations to others in acting ethically, fairly, and in doing no harm.

INDIVIDUAL   ORGANIZATION   SOCIETY & PLANET

At the base we have the **ethical responsibilities** of the organization. These are the socially responsible things companies are expected to do for reasons of principle, morality, legality, or good stewardship. Adhering to corporate values and professional ethics. Obeying the law. Meeting quality standards. Minimizing environmental impact. Sourcing goods ethically. Remunerating staff equitably. Paying tax. Being an equal opportunity employer. Creating job opportunities for young people. Providing a safe workplace. Donating to charity. Sponsoring local community activities.

For these and other such actions we should not be seeking accolades or expecting a ticker tape parade. These form part of our basic license to operate. We do the right thing simply because it is the right thing to do. Some companies, however, mistake, or even substitute, these activities for their purpose. At its worst this can take the form of "good washing"—applying a veneer of care to a business whose real motivation rises no higher than making money. Unsurprisingly, this comes across as somewhat shallow.

In any event, whilst fulfilling our social and ethical responsibilities is one key part of being a purpose-driven organization, it is not sufficient in itself.

At the next level we have our organization's **functional purposes.** These are the activities a company performs when delivering on its promise to its stakeholders. For example, a disaster relief NGO's functional purpose might relate to the speed and reliability of on-the-ground assessment and logistics. An electricity company's functional purpose is providing reliable, clean, and efficient energy. A pharmaceutical company's functional purpose may be to improve the efficacy and affordability of its medicines through research and development processes. And so on.

If a company has a valued role in the market and does it better than its competition, then differentiation and customer satisfaction tends to grow. Serving this level of purpose excellently usually brings its own reward, whether that is in the form of market share, revenue, stock price, donations, political capital, or other such results. All are good outcomes and essential to sustaining and growing our enterprises.

The problem is that many corporations see their functional purpose as the peak of their aspiration. Often this sounds something like:

To be number one in every market in which we operate.

To have the widest product selection and lowest prices.

To be the highest-quality producer in the nation.

To have the most satisfied customers.

To be an employer of choice.

All such aspirations are fine, but none really illuminate *why* that is important in the grand scheme of things. Aside from being somewhat corny, they are more summaries of a company's key performance indicators than of the greater good being pursued.

Such expressions could indeed serve as an organization's purpose statement, but only if that is the extent of their ambition.

A **higher purpose** will go to the very heart of why the organization exists, and why the world is better off as a result. It is more about the ultimate public good that it produces than the products themselves. It defines the societal aspiration the economic model is in service of. It alludes to how this difference is made and why that is important.

This kind of purpose is a higher ideal that frames and focuses, inspires and informs, all that follows—including *what* we do (i.e., our functional purpose) and *how* we ensure we go about that in a fair and appropriate manner (i.e., our ethical responsibilities).

All three levels of purpose (ethical responsibility, functional purpose, and higher purpose) need to be present in what we do. All are important and complement one another. Together they provide a moral compass that helps discern the right way of going about business. Even so, it is the higher purpose that we need clarity on first, for it provides the reason for the journey we're on—and the more elevated platform from which to see further ahead and define our opportunities more clearly. Henceforth, in this book, our primary focus is on this higher purpose.

Purpose as a Catalyst

True purpose is active not passive. It doesn't just sit around dreaming of what might happen *one day*. Rather, it challenges us to look for opportunities to start acting *today*. It is a catalyst for change.

A catalyst precipitates a desired reaction. Similarly, a great purpose attracts the attention of like-minded people and stirs those with a latent desire or potential to do more. This is critical if we're tackling a cause that really is something bigger than ourselves, for by definition we cannot do it alone. We need to draw in other talent, supporters, collaborators, and partners. Having a higher purpose does so by signaling a worthy intent, which draws others to the table.

In the early days of the coronavirus (COVID-19) pandemic, the call of public health authorities in many jurisdictions was to help "flatten the curve," to slow the spread of the virus in order to buy time for over-burdened hospitals while vaccines were being developed and distributed. Through measures such as social distancing and hygiene practices, we were asked to played our part in that collective cause. In many respects, a purpose to bring about a positive social or environmental shift follows similar principles, but in the opposite direction. Rather than delaying an unwanted development, purpose typically seeks to *bring forward* a positive change that might otherwise have taken much longer.

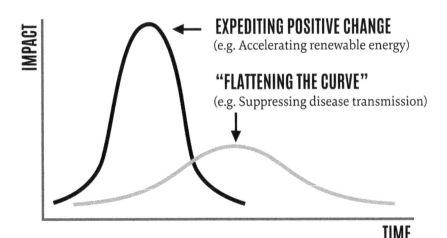

Bringing that positive change forward clearly means that more people will benefit sooner. This is our primary motivation. However, there are other important side benefits. From an enterprise perspective it accelerates value creation, thereby shortening the gap between investment and return—the so-called death valley where many well-meaning endeavors go to die. And from a change perspective it encourages the sense of urgency and momentum.

The French poet and novelist Victor Hugo, whose works include *The Hunchback of Notre-Dame* and *Les Misérables*, famously said, "there is nothing more powerful than an idea whose time has come." This notion of a worthy purpose finding its tipping point holds great appeal, being the underlying theme of many stories of transformation: the abolition of slavery, Women's suffrage, the freeing of Nelson Mandela and dismantling of apartheid, the fall of the Berlin Wall and the Iron Curtain, the launch of the first Apple computer (and later the iPhone), the invention of the World Wide Web, the signing of the UN's Millennium Declaration. These and many other developments could be thought of as ideas whose time had come. The weight of public opinion had built up behind them and triggered significant shifts in the course of society.

What constitutes the right time is an interesting question. Sometimes that moment may come by virtue of a breakthrough discovery. Sometimes it may be a confluence of external events or trends. Occasionally there may be an entrepreneur with tremendous strategic foresight patiently waiting for an anticipated time when all the conditions will be just right for making a move like a surfer waiting for the perfect wave. For a purpose-driven organization, however, the right time is typically determined more by one's own responsiveness to a need at hand than by external conditions.

If we see a pressing need, or an injustice or systemic waste, is there any virtue in waiting for a future time when things may be easier? Or is it perhaps more a matter of doing what we can with what we have—seeking to learn and build on that over time? Genuine purpose is not just a vague concept of what we might do someday in the future. It focuses attention on what we can do right now.

The choice, as some have put it, is whether we are to be a thermometer or thermostat in our chosen field. Do we simply monitor the temperature and enter the space only when conditions are favorable? Or do we get involved for the very reason that the prevailing situation is not what it should be? Indeed, that is the very nature of a higher purpose: to change the settings. This necessarily means navigating through all the messiness of an imperfect situation in order to steer it in a more positive direction. We should certainly be smart about how we do that, but let's not stand on the sidelines wondering whether or not now is the time.

Purpose produces change by removing delay, defining success, challenging the status quo, and encouraging innovation.

- **Removing delay**. If we have a worthy purpose its time has already come. Whether the purpose is to design a better way, save precious resources, avert a pending disaster, or respond to a crisis, the time is now. Nothing progresses while we're waiting for ideal conditions. Even a small or imperfect start is enough to signal intent and start ascending the learning curve. It will pay off later, if not sooner. Carpe diem!

- **Defining success**. Companies or people with a purpose are outcome oriented. They begin with the end in mind. They cut to the chase. Progress is accelerated when there is a shared vision and when they orient their efforts around the proverbial 20 percent of factors that make 80 percent of the difference. By defining success at the outset, they focus their limited resources where they are most likely to realize a breakthrough.

- **Challenging the status quo.** There is no cause to rally around if there is no discrepancy, no discontent between the way things are and the way they should be. A higher purpose shines a light on this. It may rub some people the wrong way—particularly those with a vested interest in the status quo—but it also mobilizes those who believe that there is a better way and want to be part of bringing that about. Polarization is par for the course if you're a change-maker. Be gracious toward those who may struggle with change and do your best to bring them along on the journey. But don't let opposition stall progress. There'll always be some late adopters at the back half of the change curve. They'll catch on later. Focus instead on working constructively with the innovators and early movers at the front of the curve.

- **Encouraging innovation.** Purpose creates the conditions in which innovation thrives: an important need to be met, a desire for change, focused efforts, permission to explore disruptive options, the support needed to safely "fail forward." Purpose frames the necessity that becomes the mother of invention.

If we keep seizing the *moments* in which we can make a difference, *movement* in the right direction will come. Persistence in doing so gradually builds the *momentum* needed to overturn previously intractable societal problems.

Moments → Movement → Momentum

This is how purpose-driven organizations catalyze change.

TWO

FINDING PURPOSE

"I want to put a ding in the universe."

—STEVE JOBS

S tories of how organizations found their purpose will be as varied as their contexts. Often it is effectively a case of *the purpose finding them* because of some unexpected circumstance.

This is not to say, however, that those organizations that don't yet have a fully developed sense of purpose should passively sit around waiting for it to knock on their door. There is benefit in actively going after it—either for a new endeavor before us or for deepening our understanding of a purpose we may have inherited from those who came before. In either case it may be helpful to know that such purpose may even be right in front of us, staring us in the face, but remaining unseen because we've not yet had the right lens with which to bring it into focus.

Finding purpose can either happen quickly or it could require the deepest soul searching, depending on where your organization currently stands. An established organization may face one of two broad scenarios:

1. **Revitalize** an existing purpose.
2. **(Re)cast** a new purpose.

Revitalize an Existing Purpose

If an organization's existing purpose is already relevant and instructive then there's likely no need to go looking for another. In this case it's simply a matter of recommitting and making good on that. Double down and keep forging ahead.

Some organizations seem to alter their purpose with every new strategy cycle or leadership changeover. But to do so is to misunderstand the nature of purpose altogether. We may need to pivot on strategy from time to time, and we'll certainly have to be adaptive as leaders, but the organization's reason for being should be stable and rarely, if ever, change.

As discussed earlier, an organization is basically a group of people coming together for a purpose, and if that purpose is fundamentally altered or diluted so too is its bond with its heritage and with each other. It is potentially a breaking of faith with those on whose shoulders the organization stands. It is akin to a nation changing the central tenets of its constitution, being the essential ideas that define what it stands for, bind it together and imbue it with a sense of meaning, identity, and cohesion over time. That may not be such a big deal for a mass producer of widgets, but it is for an organization that has faithfully served a higher purpose for decades prior. While there is no rule that says an organization can't change its purpose, as with a house, you'd need a very good reason to start removing or re-engineering the foundation. In most cases it's far better to reinforce and build upon what's already there.

An organization that frequently alters its purpose is not purpose-driven. To be indecisive about one's unique role in the bigger picture is to become lost within it. To stand only for what's trending now is to fade with the next cycle. To treat purpose as a variable, a tool, is to be short sighted and stuck in the realm of the tactical. If the road to success really is *consistency of purpose*, then an organization that's distracted or double minded in this regard is caught in a loop, always moving but never really progressing in any meaningful sense.

It may be that, for whatever reason, the organization's existing purpose has become somewhat tired or tarnished over time. Perhaps subsequent generations of leaders or staff have drifted away from the bold ambition that gave birth to the enterprise. It may be that the purpose has become somewhat blasé in its familiarity or because of the lip service it has been paid in years prior. Perhaps its framing was too transactional, too self-serving, to have any real power to inspire. Perhaps the company is recovering from a crisis of some kind, having thought only of survival in recent times.

In such cases we may indeed need to reconnect with, or revitalize, our existing purpose.

To do so, we need to take a step back before we can go forward. When we lose something of value, we retrace our steps to find it. When someone wants us to look at their outfit or car, we instinctively take a step back to get a better view. Likewise when standing too close to a problem, we instinctively take a step back so we might regain a sense of perspective and of the whole. The same applies for those seeking to reclaim or revitalize an existing purpose. If there was an earlier time when the organization was genuinely driven by its purpose and was firing on all cylinders, it's helpful to go back there in our minds, reidentify with those who were there and seek to understand at a deeper level why that season was so pivotal.

This is not about dwelling in the past or yearning for the good old days. It is not driving by the rear vision mirror. Rather, it's about reconnecting with the big idea that propelled the organization forward in the first place. That which attracted support and fueled its growth.

It is not necessarily looking at *what* the organization did in terms of activities or methods, but rather *why* its purpose, its reason for being and the underlying need it was serving, was so powerful. The times will have changed since then, but often the core societal needs and success principles are more enduring.

Having reconnected with that power source, the key then is to give it fresh expression for one's contemporary context. Sometimes in the wordsmithing, but always in action. Finding innovative ways in which to bring that to life in line with current community or market needs. The purpose itself might be twenty, fifty, or a hundred years old, but that in no way prevents us from using creativity, entrepreneurship or the latest technology or scientific knowledge in advancing it in our day. In this way the organization can be both true to itself *and* continually moving forward.

As with a tree, the health and stability of an organization depends on the depth of its roots. Deep roots will help determine how high it can grow, the abundance of fruit it will produce, and the extent to which it can remain resilient through the droughts or storms that inevitably come. We should never underestimate the value of remaining true in this regard for, "the secret of success is constancy to purpose."

We can get a sense of this through the purpose statements of iconic organizations who've remained true to who they are over many years and yet still continue to innovate and effect positive change. Consider these purpose statements:

> "Using the power of science, exploration, education and storytelling to illuminate and protect the wonder of our world." (National Geographic)

"To develop leaders who will one day make a global difference." (Harvard University)

"The increase and diffusion of knowledge." (The Smithsonian)

"To build healthier lives, free of cardiovascular diseases and stroke." (American Heart Association)

"The maintenance of international peace and security." (United Nations)

Purposes such as these are enduring. They are as relevant today as they were generations ago. They go to the heart of the matter and need no tweaking. They would only lose their potency if they were redirected, diluted, or conformed to the trending jargon of the day. The authenticity of these iconic organizations arises from their continuing connection with their foundation story, the integrity with which they have been pursued, and the faithfulness of those who've picked up the baton and continued these legacies. They benefit more from recommitting to their founding purpose and by finding new ways to bring these to life in contemporary circumstances than by altering the purpose itself.

The greatest impact and meaning arises when we combine integrity (consistency of purpose) with innovation (in how we bring them to life).

(Re)cast a New Purpose

There are situations in which a new purpose may be needed, most obviously for a proposed new endeavor. In some cases, however, it may also be that the purpose of an existing organization needs to be fundamentally reconceived. For example, an organization that's only ever really served itself might need to find a more beneficial raison d'être, one that focuses more on the customers and society on which it depends. Or perhaps it may be an instance of the proverbial sword manufacturer seeking to switch its operations to plowshares, which is to say, an organization that previously caused harm now desiring to do good.

There are many ways in which organizations discover their raison d'être. Some stumble upon it; others have it thrust upon them. Regardless, there is value in outlining what a more intentional approach might look like. One that gives greater order and depth to our thinking—while also keeping it simple.

The clue is in the nature of purpose itself, which goes to the very essence of the organization. It is the purest, most concentrated, most elementary articulation of the most fundamental question of all: Why are we here as an entity? It follows therefore that the process to identify or recast purpose will often be one of distillation.

In its simplest form, purpose can be progressively revealed or refined through three filtering questions:

1. What is the **real need** to be met?
2. What is the **confident hope** of change to be had in this regard?
3. What **responsibility** do we accept in this?

The fundamental need the organization is meeting is the *subject* of its purpose. The confidence and capability we have to meet those needs represents the relative *strength* of that purpose. The depth at which we accept responsibility for our particular role in this quest is the extent to which we'll have an authentic and unwavering *sense* of purpose.

1. SUBJECT OF PURPOSE:
The real need to be met.

2. STRENGTH OF PURPOSE:
A basis for confidence.

3. SENSE OF PURPOSE:
Acceptance of responsibility.

Let's break this down.

The Real Need to Be Met

"It's not about you." So begins the opening chapter of one of the world's best-selling books, *The Purpose Driven Life*. Although Rick Warren's exhortation is more about one's personal outlook on life, the same principles can apply to organizations.

If we want to be part of something bigger than ourselves and make a difference in the world, we'll never find that focus by looking only inward. Purpose must be about the greater good if it is to have any broader appeal or influence. In contrast, to be self-serving in a world that owes us nothing, is a zero-sum game, and ultimately exhausting.

Purpose is about a need to be met (or problem to be solved, or new height to be reached) for the benefit of others. It is not about the product or service you're selling. Without such a need there can be no purpose, for it would have no beneficial outcome. And without someone to serve, there is no market or constituency.

Walmart's stated purpose is to "help people live better and renew the planet while building thriving, resilient communities."[1] It sells tens of thousands of different products in every store but that is merely a way of achieving its goal, not an end in itself. There's something deeper at play: a business model that is designed to make those products more affordable and accessible to everyone, including those on lower incomes. Beyond that its intent is also to create jobs, be inclusive, sponsoring local community activities, reshape supply chains, and adopt more sustainable practices. It's all these elements, bound together by a higher purpose, that bring about the positive societal impact Walmart wants to have. In the process it also makes money as a result.

Products are a *means* of serving. Profit is the *outcome* of a purpose well-served.

There is no shortage of need around us. For the purpose-driven, it is a an opportunity-rich environment so to speak. But which particular need should your team focus on? That's a question only you can answer.

Needs are situated within (and may even be the result of) a broader context. In essence they represent a gap between what is, and what could or should be. These unmet needs stand in the way of a better future for those customers or citizens. The purpose of the enterprise is to address the needs in a way that unlocks that future potential. To do so one must

1. **identify** the most important needs that persist in your market or sphere of influence (i.e., your organization's context);

2. **select** the one need (or cluster of related needs) whose resolution would have the greatest positive impact *and* which best align with your values, aspirations, culture, and core competencies;

3. **translate** that problem into a purpose statement that addresses the very heart of the matter: the customer's deepest need or the root cause of the problem at hand. This defines our role in the

resolution of the issue and begins to spark the imagination as to how we might outwork that purpose in practice. Whether we subsequently nail the solution ourselves, or simply make some contribution, all progress in this direction will be valuable.

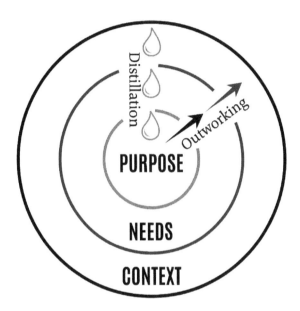

If our purpose is distilled in this way, it becomes more potent and more instructive about where we should focus our attention. Given the clear alignment between the need, the context, and our role, our efforts are more likely to have a positive ripple effect.

This broadly corresponds to the motive, meaning, and opportunity analogy. Motive arises when our intrinsic drivers find a resonant context within which we are disposed to act. Opportunity is found at the intersection of an unmet external need and the internal set of capabilities we can bring to the challenge. Meaning comes from being part of a positive transformation, both in addressing immediate needs and bringing about a more enduring, systemic change. That is, making a difference.

Picking up again on the Google example, its purpose statement sits in the context of a rapidly digitizing world with rapidly expanding volumes of data. It focuses on the need to make information more accessible in such an environment. And it frames its purpose quite specifically as better *organizing* that information. When Google's purpose statement was first crafted back in the day, it could easily have been something like "to provide a superior search engine." But by going deeper to address an underlying need that is likely to become even more important across applications and time, it set itself up for ongoing relevance and increasing opportunity.

Zeroing in on an underlying need in this way provides the first element of an organizational reason for being: the subject of your purpose. Now you have a clear focus.

A Basis for Confidence

"There's a fine line between fishing and just standing on the shore like an idiot."

—Steven Wright

Nobody sets out on a hopeless journey. They require some basis for confidence that the desired end is possible, even if it is stretching.

If we have a purpose, we also have a gap, a chasm to cross, separating what is from what could be. And since no one can tell the future, there is always at least some degree of uncertainty or ambiguity. And yet somehow the genuinely purpose-driven seem to possess a degree of confidence, managing through that tension between what is known (facts) and what is yet to be seen, understood, or created (future). The connector between these is faith.

Faith may seem like an unorthodox concept in a book about strategy. It may even seem incongruous to an evidence-based mindset. And yet, faith and evidence work hand in hand. We combine them all the time. When we set a vision and step forward in that direction, when we ideate about the best answer to a problem and then seek to explore that possibility, when we hire someone we don't know on the basis of another's recommendation, when we enter an emerging new market, when we make an investment, when we pay the cheapest airfare available before boarding a 180-ton steel tube that flies through the air at 500 knots, 35,000 feet above an ocean, we are practicing faith. In each case we have some end in mind, some facts we can rely on, and other elements we can't see or know for certain but in which we choose to place our confidence, for often that is the only way we can move forward. We take those elements on faith.

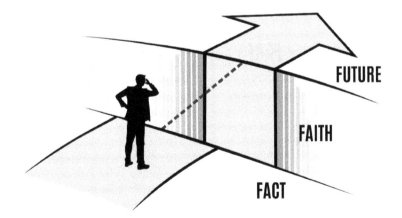

Faith is defined as, "complete trust or confidence in someone or something. A strongly held belief." (Oxford Dictionary) or, "assurance of things hoped for, a conviction of things not seen" (Heb. 11:1 ASV).

This is the way of just about every leader, innovator, entrepreneur, or social change agent who successfully transforms the order of things for the better. When their stories are told in hindsight, they make great case studies that may seem as though the outcome was always inevitable. At the outset of their journeys, and in many points in between, however, there will have been private moments of doubt—usually overcome by a doubling down on the belief that first led them to understand that real change, growth, and impact was possible. In their mind's eye they saw a future not yet realized but which they believed could be. They set out exploring this future in the hope and belief that a way could be found.

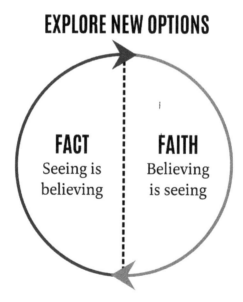

EXPLORE NEW OPTIONS

FACT
Seeing is
believing

FAITH
Believing
is seeing

What we know to be fact today came about because someone earlier learned a lesson by stepping forward in faith. Someone who, despite the imperfect knowledge they had at the time, nevertheless proceeded with a conviction that they could rely on certain forces, principles, or abilities to help them find a solution. That experience of moving forward in *faith* produced the next set of *facts* upon which to stand. It is as logical and progressive as walking by putting one foot in front of the other. As Pablo Picasso said, "I am always doing that which I cannot do, in order that I may learn how to do it."

We see the same principle at work in other familiar concepts such as visionary leadership, the growth mindset, and entrepreneurship. It is the idea of learning by doing, getting ahead of the pack, and developing strategic options, all of which point to the need to take considered steps forward into unknown territory if we are to find an advantage and make progress. (Doubly so when one's purpose involves tackling a stubborn societal challenge crying out for new answers).

"If we knew what we were doing, we wouldn't call it research."
—Albert Einstein

In the movie, *Indiana Jones & The Last Crusade,* Harrison Ford's character, an archaeologist, is on a quest to find the Holy Grail. There's a scene in which he's standing on one side of a chasm with an urgent need to get to the other. Many who'd gone before had failed. The cryptic clues in a notebook Dr. Jones was following suggested there was an invisible bridge across the abyss. Naturally, he hesitated in stepping out onto an object that he couldn't yet see or comprehend, but this was just one of those situations when the proof of his hypothesis could only come after he demonstrated faith. He stepped out and did indeed make it across. It was, at the same time, both a leap of faith and a considered move. If Dr. Jones was to fulfill his quest, he had no choice but to move forward. He had the clues from the notebook, which had proved reliable up to that point, and the sense of something solid underfoot when he put his first foot forward into the void. Though the data was incomplete, and success was by no means guaranteed, these elements in combination provided enough confidence for the scientist to act.

The problem for those who'd come before Dr. Jones was never that there was no way across. Rather it was that they either did not have the eyes to see it or the conviction needed to step forward into the unfamiliar.

> *"Faith is taking the first step even when you don't see*
> *the whole staircase."*
> —Dr Martin Luther King Jr.

Faith is often required of us when negotiating the gap between what we presently know and are yet to realize—between fact and future. We too will need to identify our invisible bridge at many points in the purpose journey, and place weight on that.

Faith itself doesn't achieve anything. There's no mysterious power in it. It doesn't make us superhuman. The power (or powerlessness as the case may be) is in the *object* of our faith. Faith is simply a choice to trust in the thing that has the authority, capacity, or strength to make the difference. It connects our purpose to that force. Or to put it another way, we must be clear on what we are choosing to place our faith *in* before we can have genuine hope *for* some greater outcome. The stronger the object of that faith, the greater the strength of our purpose.

Confidence in oneself is fine but it does have its limits, beyond which we may find the kind of hubris that blinds us to what's really going on. Optimism is a great attitude to have, but it holds no sway over the external forces we face. Ultimately the most effective posture of all is placing our faith in something that is trustworthy and of greater strength and influence than we can possess ourselves.

When it comes to developing strategy, we often focus on observable short- or mid-term trends. They ebb and flow, come and go. We time our moves to take advantage of those factors within narrower timeframes. When it comes to developing a plan, we focus more on risks or assumptions. These also have their place, applying a negative screen on our present choices to ensure we've thought through what could potentially go wrong. Purpose however sits at a higher level and focuses on a longer-term outcome than a particular strategy or plan. Hence it requires a bigger frame. We need a more enduring source of conviction for the long road ahead—a journey in which much of what we'll encounter cannot be foreseen. If we're to step into that future with confidence, we must know that we're tapping into something that empowers us with a genuine prospect of success.

Organizations vary in how (or whether) they incorporate the object of their faith into their purpose statement. In some cases, it will be quite explicit. Consider for example, the mission statement of Intel: "To utilize the power of Moore's Law to bring smart, connected devices to every person on earth."

Here the company's object of faith, or the basis for confidence, comes from Intel cofounder Gordon Moore's forecast that the computing power of a chip will likely double every twenty-four months (later reduced to eighteen months). This has since proven to be a fair prediction given the exponential increases we've seen since Moore's Law was first posited in 1965. Alongside that, costs have come down, providing sufficient confidence for Intel to keep innovating and pushing into new territory all these years later.

Google's mission statement is somewhat similar in nature, although it's object of faith is more implicit. If it is to "organize the world's information and make it universally accessible and useful," it must have some confidence that that is indeed possible over the long run. We might deduce that it saw a future in which the increasing digitization of information, and the use of algorithms would make that goal increasingly possible so long as they stayed at the forefront of that curve. Hence it too leans into the emerging future with the assurance that ways can be found.

This same principle also applies to those that are literally (and not just nominally or culturally) faith-based. Ordinary people and organizations doing extraordinary things to improve life for others, being informed and driven by personal faith. A significant number of the world's nonprofits would fit in this category, ranging from international NGOs to social service organizations to local churches to grassroots social change agents. Examples of such purpose statements are:

> "To preach the gospel of Jesus Christ and to meet human needs in His name without discrimination." (Salvation Army)

> "To share the Gospel and extend the love of Christ . . . and teach Christians and non-Christians alike how to enjoy everyday life by applying biblical principles in all they do." (Joyce Meyer Ministries)

> "To know Christ, be the church, and serve our community with a message of hope, truth and love." (Edge Church, Australia)

In these cases the object of faith is a person: Jesus Christ. Though each of these organizations operate in different contexts, with different forms of outreach, their expressions of purpose reside within the same overarching biblical message, the gospel (meaning "good news"). This message might be summarized thus:

> God is the author and designer of life. He has a purpose and plan for every person. He knows, loves, and calls us into that by name.

But we were also given a free will. With that we ignored God and went our own way. As a result, we messed things up, both in our own lives and in the world we were meant to care for. However, out of love, God sent His son Jesus to show us what He is like, how to live, and to offer forgiveness—thereby opening a way back into right relationship with Him (i.e., by us placing our faith in Christ). In doing so we are given a fresh start, being renewed from the inside out, and are reconnected into a much bigger story. We begin to see things from a new perspective and experience more of life as it was intended. We find new purpose in serving and seeking the best for others—extending the same love we have ourselves received.

As in any other case, the strength of such a purpose rests on the validity of that in which one's trust has been placed. If this is just fabricated, man-made religion with no substance to it, then perhaps it is as Karl Marx put it, merely "the opium of the people."[2] In stating the case for atheism Richard Dawkins went so far as to say, "the universe that we observe has precisely the properties we should expect if there is, at bottom, no design, no purpose, no evil, no good, nothing but pitiless indifference."[3] If that were the case, faith in Christ would have no power to transform lives, nor any longevity. Conversely, if this gospel is true, it would be the most profoundly important and transformative frame of all, a greater narrative within which our own identity and purpose may be found. It might be that, as Billy Graham put it, "Christ's message when he was upon the earth was revolutionizing and understandable. His words were simple and yet profound. . . . The (people) who followed Him were unique in their generation. They turned the world upside down because their hearts had been turned right side up."[4]

"We look at this Son and see the God who cannot be seen.
We look at this Son and see God's original purpose in everything
created. For everything, absolutely everything... got started in him
and finds its purpose in him."

—Colossians 1:15-16 MSG

Whatever perspective or sector we're coming from, the point is the same. If we're to embark on a bold purpose, seeking to change the order of things for the better, we first need to have sound reason to believe that it is possible, an authentic basis for our conviction and hope. Ideally, we should have the most meaningful, powerful, and reliable object of faith available. Our prospects for success are closely tied to the validity of that in which we have (explicitly or implicitly) placed our faith. So, in formulating our purpose, let us think deeply about that and be intentional from the very outset.

We need to ask ourselves, "what is it that we are essentially placing our faith in? What long-run principle, force, ability, or person(s) are we ultimately relying upon to prevail? What is it that we are "hitching our wagon" to? It can be a hard question to answer, one that first requires deep reflection, and then some up-front choices that may be polarizing for some. But, if we're able to find clarity and confidence in this, it will only strengthen our purpose, our resilience, and our prospects.

Acceptance of Responsibility

"The price of greatness is responsibility."
—Winston Churchill

It's not enough to simply articulate a purpose. We must serve it as well.

A purpose statement that just sits passively on our website or annual report is less than useful. Indeed, it may only serve to fuel the discontent of staff and stakeholders who see the discrepancy between the articulated intent and any meaningful progress in that direction.

If the stated purpose is not being acted upon, there is no momentum, nothing to join in, nothing of any substance by which to be inspired. There is no credibility, no real impact. Just empty words.

The final step in our search for purpose must be to *take responsibility* for pursuing that which was identified as being both worthy and possible. It is only then that we can truly say that we have a *sense* of purpose.

It can be a sobering moment, for it is also the first step in what may be a long and challenging journey ahead. It is the point at which we put our money where our mouth is, not just once but every day and at every decision point where that purpose could be advanced—even if only one inch at a time.

There are many things outside our control. But there are two basic choices that we do have. To accept conditions as they currently are, or to accept responsibility for our role in bringing about positive change. If we commit to the latter, we get to be part of the solution—even if that entails difficulty. Until then we are merely observers or passengers.

*"In any given moment we have two options: to step forward into
growth or step back into safety."*

—Abraham Maslow

Taking responsibility is the difference between pointing to a purpose and genuinely possessing one. Between a follower and a leader. Between dreaming and doing. Between potential and progress.

Taking responsibility is a conscious pre-decision to step out and pursue that purpose in and through every circumstance. It is to lead. Often that will come naturally, with the right path being apparent and the next step forward an intuitive one. Sometimes however it may mean committing to the harder route over the more expedient one. At other junctures we may have to choose to go against the flow of what everyone else is doing in order to find a new and better way. In all cases being purpose driven requires that we remain true to that which we have said we will stand for.

*"The most difficult thing is the decision to act,
the rest is merely tenacity."*

—Amelia Earhart

The Prize and the Price

To think of oneself as a purpose-driven organization or leader is easy. Most everyone has a desire for significance and for making a difference. We can be wonderfully optimistic or even tend toward romanticism at the outset of the journey. We might imagine ourselves cracking the case on those tough societal issues, setting things right, seeing all prosper, and turning up for our award ceremony. But the day-to-day experience is not so ideal. Things get tough, messy, and frustrating. We make mistakes, miss forecasts, face opposition, and become weary at times. The pursuit of a purpose has real costs, difficulties and risks attached to it. Taking responsibility requires counting the costs.

> *"There is nothing more difficult to take in hand, more perilous to conduct, or more uncertain in its success, than to take the lead in the introduction of a new order of things."*
>
> —Niccolò Machiavelli

Ultimately the value of something is determined by the price someone is prepared to pay for it. Something of great value will invariably require a substantial exchange. The more noble the purpose, the more challenging the issue, the loftier the ambition, the rarer the prize, the higher the price.

When building a new home or starting a new venture, one not only considers the ultimate value of the finished product (the prize) but also calculates the resources needed to accomplish that endeavor (the price). If we're wise, we'll factor in some margin for error to accommodate delays or overruns. It would be foolish to even start if we're unwilling to pay the associated cost.

In the case of organizational purposes counting the cost is not simply about a financial business case. Or even necessarily about money at all. It is being clear in our minds (individually and collectively) that the outcome being sought is worthy of all that may be involved in its pursuit. How important is this to us, really? What would we be prepared to forego or endure or invest to see that come about?

If you count the cost in advance, you won't be tortured along the way as to whether it's all worth it. You will already know that it is. You will be free to focus more fully on the prize itself, being better placed to see it through.

> *"Life is difficult. This is a great truth, one of the greatest truths.*
> *It is a great truth because once we truly see this truth,*
> *we transcend it. Once we truly know that life is difficult—*
> *once we truly understand and accept it—then life is no*
> *longer difficult. Because once it is accepted, the fact that*
> *life is difficult no longer matters."*
>
> —Scott Peck

This really says two things. First, that the purpose journey is not for the faint-hearted or double-minded. Secondly, that the purpose we've committing to had better be one of genuine value, meaning and impact. One worthy of the price.

From an enterprise perspective, the very difficulties that made the journey so challenging may in fact represent an advantage: a deterrent or barrier to entry to competitors - and the first-mover's opportunity to survey and inhabit prime positions in the new territory.

Passion

One often hears advice along the lines of "if you've found your passion, you've found your purpose." That could be either the best or worst counsel you'll receive, depending on your understanding of passion. The Oxford dictionary defines *passion* as "strong and barely controllable emotion" or "an intense desire or enthusiasm for something." This is the most common contemporary use of the term in both everyday conversation and in literature about finding purpose. That is entirely understandable for indeed we do need a strong sense of engagement in the cause we're taking up. We want to feel that there's some alignment between the need at hand and our own interests and talents. It is a natural expectation to have.

The problem arises when the problem or need we're trying to address outlasts or overwhelms our emotional interest. We might become discouraged by the obstacles we strike along the way or become distracted by a new passion. In both cases we may find that the basis of our initial commitment falls short of the determination and endurance needed to finish the journey.

The Latin root of *passion* is *passio* or *pati*, meaning "to suffer." At Easter we might see a movie or play entitled *The Passion of the Christ*. You might have heard of artists suffering for their art or of the expression "freedom is not free," referring to the military cost of defending liberty. An intense desire and suffering sometimes go together. The deep commitment to do what it takes on the one hand (even though the option is always there to give up and walk away) and the subsequent breakthrough on the other (an outcome which could not have been achieved without having endured and pushed through) are two sides of the same coin. When the purpose journey gets tough, the inherent difference in these forms of passion will lead us on different paths:

Passion as **emotional enthusiasm**	Passion as a **weighty commitment**
(Latin: enthusiasmus)	(Latin: passio, pati)
Arises from an instinctive idea and therefore can be more fleeting.	Arises from a considered, firm decision and therefore is more resolute.
Pursuit of personal satisfaction.	Pursuit of benefit for others.
Activity-oriented.	Outcome-oriented.
Focuses principally on the prize.	Considers both the prize and the price.

The intent in pointing out this difference is not to devalue an emotional interest or enthusiasm, but to ensure that we've properly considered the challenges before us and are prepared to go the distance.

In the context of an organization where there are multiple people involved (perhaps thousands) and serious investments being made, one's personal passion is too ephemeral or fleeting a basis on which to guide corporate efforts over the long term. The sense of purpose may have started with the founder(s), but it also needs to be embraced more widely if the organization is to maintain its shape, growth, and impact.

People who have been immersed in serious social challenges like the grinding poverty we may see in urban slums, the distress of children with an abusive parent, or environmental challenges like the alarm of a warming planet are generally driven more by the weightiness of the need than by personal interest. Although it is a more solemn form of commitment, this also provides a deeper, more enduring, and more grounded sense of purpose. Why? Because:

- It brings to the fore that which is truly important.
- It provides a much clearer view of what real impact and progress looks like.
- People can bring both their heart *and* head (emotional *and* rational selves) to the challenge at hand.
- It is not peculiar to the interests of one founder, or a small number of people. It opens the purpose up to more people, perpetually, over years to come.
- It compels us to persist. We are, therefore, much more likely to achieve advances along the way.
- We appreciate the value of the gains made because of the price paid, challenges overcome, and being "in the trenches" together. This results in a deeper form of satisfaction and cultural bonding.

- We grow as people. In character, resilience, wisdom, connection. As with muscle these attributes only grow through the exercising of responsibility, the lifting of weight, consistency of endeavor.

This is not to say a sense of purpose should be unduly burdensome—some joyless or crushing weight of expectation to achieve the impossible. Accepting responsibility does not mean we carry the whole load by ourselves. On the contrary. Although we may be cognizant of the gravity of the situation, we balance that with a corresponding acceptance that we cannot possibly solve it all by ourselves. Hence, we seek out that part of the wider solution in which our talents and resources could indeed make a meaningful contribution—and run with that. Rarely are we accepting responsibility for the whole problem, but rather, a particular role in helping address it. One in which we can bring the best of ourselves to join with the unique gifts of others. Finding this sweet spot in our understanding of our purpose is energizing not onerous. It is a responsibility we grab with both hands not only because it is needed, but also because it aligns with what we can contribute, and because we can envisage the difference that could be made if we succeed.

Google does not seek to *produce* all the world's information, only to help *organize* it in order to make it more accessible. TED does not seek to *develop* its own world-changing ideas so much as *spread* those researchers and thought-leaders want to share. Harvard does not seek to *change* the world by itself, only to *develop* the future leaders who could. Each of these purposes identifies and commits to a specific role within a bigger context and ecosystem of players who each play their part. Their chosen role is valid not vague, feasible not futile, liberating not laborious.

The virtue is not in the difficulty itself, but in the stepping forward and taking of responsibility for an outcome that would make a real difference for others. It is in the focus, resolve, and persistence that overcomes the hurdles one by one and which produces the organizational mettle, resilience, creativity, hope, and trust needed to break new ground.

> *"We choose to go to the Moon in this decade and do the other*
> *things, not because they are easy, but because they are hard,*
> *because that goal will serve to organize and measure the best of*
> *our energies and skills, because that challenge is one that we are*
> *willing to accept, one we are unwilling to postpone,*
> *and one which we intend to win...."*

—John F. Kennedy

1. SUBJECT OF PURPOSE:
The real need to be met.

2. STRENGTH OF PURPOSE:
A basis for confidence.

3. SENSE OF PURPOSE:
Acceptance of responsibility.

So, there we have it. The three dimensions of an organizational purpose:

The *subject* of purpose is an important need to be met, or problem to be solved, or better future to unlock.

The *strength* of purpose is a basis for confidence, a reasoned faith, that this end can indeed be achieved.

The *sense* of purpose is the acceptance of responsibility for our particular role in meeting a need, and the determination to see that through to the best of our ability.

THREE

PURPOSE FINDING YOU

Before moving on it is worth highlighting a special purpose, one that is perhaps the most profound type of lifework or mission: a calling.

A calling has all the qualities described earlier with one critical difference. With a calling we are not the ones who identify the need to solve or the role to play. These are given by another. All we have to do is decide whether or not we will take on that responsibility. As the catchphrase from the *Mission Impossible* series goes: "Your mission, should you choose to accept it, is to . . ."

A calling implies there is a Who behind the Why. That someone issues the call. Someone whose interests we place above our own and whose cause or authority carries weight with us. Someone whose call is worth heeding, even though it may require risk, sacrifice, or cut across the path we had previously envisaged for ourselves.

This is perhaps most starkly illustrated in times of war. The need is not one we went looking for—it came to us. We may not even have thought of it as a possibility in our lifetime. But even so the need is compelling, superseding whatever our personal plans might otherwise have been. The who issuing the call in this case might be the government of the day (via a call up) or it might be the collective voice of innocent people in desperate need of defense, in which case we may choose to sign up. Either way when someone goes off to war, they're accepting that call and being commissioned (read: *co-missioned*) along with others into the resolution of that great challenge.

Many in the humanitarian, health, or social service spheres started out after sensing some knock at the door of their hearts after witnessing or experiencing a tragedy or injustice. Maybe they saw something on the news or on an overseas trip or in a chance encounter or even in their own family. In pursuit of righting some wrong, many subsequently formed charities or agencies or social enterprises to scale up the positive impact they wanted to have. As those initiatives grew, others joined, taking on the organizational mission as their own. That is to say, they too accepted the call.

> *"You are not here in the world for yourself. You have been sent here for others. The world is waiting for you!"*
>
> —Catherine Booth

The concept of a calling is also (and originally) associated with faith. In this case the who, the source of the call into some vocation or undertaking, is God. Perhaps not via an audible voice or dramatic epiphany, but some kind of deep and persistent drawing in a certain direction, a beckoning from beyond themselves. First and foremost, the call is to follow Him. But thereafter there may be a sense of being sent or commissioned into some endeavor—typically in service of others, something they might not otherwise have thought of or chosen for themselves. As unlikely as this may sound to some, the fact is that such a sense of calling became the driving force for many of the purpose-driven advances we might take for granted today. From the founding of kindergartens to universities (including Oxford and Harvard for example). Christians with a sense of calling made major contributions to the scientific method (Copernicus, Galileo, Francis Bacon, Isaac Newton) and individual sciences such as chemistry (Antoine Lavoisier, Robert Boyle). This also extends to innovations like nursing (Florence Nightingale) and vaccination (Louis Pasteur). And from the printing press (Johannes Gutenberg) to computing (Charles Babbage). There were champions in many movements seeking social justice, such as the abolition of slavery (Wilbur Wilberforce) and the Civil Rights movement (Dr. Martin Luther King). People with a similar sense of calling were at the forefront of many great innovations and moments in history.

Even in relatively secular Western societies, a significant proportion of nonprofit organizations were founded on this sense of calling. Perhaps more to the point, today there are millions of ordinary people who would perceive their vocation or enterprise to be such a calling.

> *"For I know the plans I have for you," says the Lord. "*
> *They are plans for good and not for disaster,*
> *to give you a future and a hope."*
>
> —Jeremiah 29:11 NLT

A calling is especially potent for within it we see many of the elements described previously, all bundled up into one crystallizing and mobilizing idea; a need to meet; someone to serve; a role to play; meaning, motive and opportunity; a direction to move in; a basis for confidence; an idea whose time has come. The primary driver of success then becomes unwavering commitment to that call, a "long obedience in the same direction."[1] This activates the cumulative effects of focus, persistence, learning, adaptation, innovation, character- and relationship-building, credibility, and trust. All of which increase the prospects of breakthrough and growth.

An interesting example of the bond between purpose, impact, and increase is found in the story of the YMCA especially over its first one hundred years or so. The YMCA experienced rapid growth around the world, not only because of the extraordinary catalog of innovations and leaders it developed and the community impact it had, but because it managed to do so as a grassroots community movement of millions of people from all corners and cultures of the globe with only the barest of coordination—because they were all bound by a shared purpose and values. It's also remarkable for its longevity, with a like-mindedness being sustained from one generation to the next for more than 175 years and counting.

From its founding by a group of twelve young people meeting in a factory dorm room in London in 1844, the YMCA **grew** rapidly across Europe, North America, Australia, and elsewhere. By 1910 some eight thousand YMCAs had been formed. Not branch offices of a global entity, but eight thousand independently founded and governed organizations, all subscribing to the same sense of calling, all full of people taking responsibility for their local communities and putting themselves forward to serve principally as volunteers. They were all essentially crowdfunding their own resources to lease or construct facilities and to run programs for the development and well-being of young people. Such rapid growth would be remarkable enough in today's context. But this was in the Victorian era, in the days of sailing ships and telegraph—not airlines and the Internet. It was a social movement in the most genuine, gritty, and analogue sense of that term.

The YMCA story is even more remarkable in terms of social **impact**. In going about its mission, it developed many of the world's most popular sports, such as basketball, volleyball, softball, and futsal. They invented group swimming lessons and youth work, physical education, summer camps, and after-school programs. The list goes on. Then there is an astonishing history of large-scale support services for soldiers, POWs, victims of war, and migrants. The YMCA reached millions, including those on the frontlines, with some fifteen hundred YMCA huts in or near the trenches of World War 1.

There are many famous changemakers who developed their leadership skills at the YMCA, ranging from US presidents (Reagan and Carter) to Nobel Peace Prize laureates (such as Henri Dunant who later founded the Red Cross). The full list of credits is a long one. But perhaps even more important than its headline outputs is the position the Y holds with countless people around the world as a safe, welcoming, and life-giving space in their communities, a place of acceptance and care, and of opportunities to grow as a person in body, mind, and spirit, as its mission states. Many people look back on their time at the YMCA as one of the most pivotal in their lives. And they stay connected. Even today, around a million people across 120 countries continue to volunteer at the Y every year.

The pervasive sense of **calling** and possibility across the YMCA movement in its booming early years is evident in the books written by those who were part of it. Despite the somewhat formal language of the 1800s and early 1900s, two underlying messages consistently come through. First, the writers were just about popping out of their skins with wonder at the extraordinary growth and impact being realized. They had a clear sense that they were participants in something much greater than themselves. The other is a repeated appeal from those witnessing these things: that subsequent generations of leaders ensure that they remain true to the calling and not allow themselves to drift. For example, Dr.

John R. Mott (one of the key global leaders of the time and another recipient of the Nobel Peace Prize) wrote the foreword for the book celebrating the YMCA's one hundred-year anniversary. These words are reportedly the last he wrote prior to his death a few weeks later:

> "The first century has been one of pioneering, of pathfinding, and of adventure. It has been a period of entering doors opened by God. It has been a period of secure foundation laying; the foundations which have been laid have been broad, deep, solid and capable of sustaining a great superstructure. It has been a century of seed sowing and watering, at times with tears, also of diligent cultivation.... of confronting successive generations of youth with the central figure of the ages, the Lord Jesus Christ. Herein has been the hidden source from which have flowed the power and fruitfulness of the YMCA."[2]

No doubt, over that first century and its second, there will also have been many trials, wrong turns and failures accompanying the advances. There was likely mission drift at times, and dilution of its founding vision and values. That is always a possibility in a diverse, globally dispersed movement of volunteers and staff, and over such a long period. When imperfect people get together in any organization, even one with high ideals, mistakes are bound to happen. Thankfully, perfection is not the point. In the end what matters more is a continual reconnection with our calling, a picking up of the baton from wherever we may have dropped it and continuing to run the race with perseverance. To do so is to reinject the sense of drive and possibility that our organizations set out with. It is to remain part of and to perpetuate the long arc of change that bends toward justice.

The secret of success is constancy to purpose.

PART II

STRATEGIC CLARITY

"The step before genius is clarity."

—ALBERT EINSTEIN

Once we're clear on our purpose, our minds inevitably turn to how we might bring that about. We begin thinking about the moves that might help us close the gap between our starting point and our aspiration. If the goal is an audacious one, or if we're contending with particularly complex or dynamic situations, the mind may boggle as to where to start. Somehow, we must gain some perspective, some bearings by which we can navigate and get some order in our thinking. Only then can we even begin to contemplate what a more detailed strategy might look like. That is, we first need the *clarity* that precedes any kind of strategic breakthrough.

In this part of the book, we explore how we might penetrate the obscurity and get to a place where we can see, choose, and articulate our direction more clearly. This is the task of *strategic thinking*. We'll progressively build an understanding of how to

- adopt a strategic thinking mindset (or **elevate our view**),
- **frame the opportunity** before us,
- identify the right questions to ask and answer (the **turning points**), and
- **connect the dots** by developing a narrative that makes plain the way forward.

FOUR

ELEVATE YOUR VIEW

*"To succeed it is necessary to accept the world as it is
and rise above it."*

—MICHAEL KORDA

If we want to work *on* the business and not just *in* the business, we must first lift ourselves *above* the business. We must find a higher perspective from which to get a sense of the scope and shape of the whole. It's important to have a mental vantage point from which we might see over or around the fog to where we want to be on the other side. And from which we might identify some peaks or landmarks by which to plot our way through. We can't anticipate everything that will happen as we step forward but there are some things we can think through and be prepared for beforehand. Being clear on the angle from which we'll come at this and having a few key coordinates makes all the difference.

Thinking Strategically

*"You can't solve a problem on the same level that it was created.
You have to rise above it to the next level."*

—Albert Einstein

There are any number of books or articles that might guide us in developing a business plan. There are conferences and reports to tell us about the latest trends and research. We may already have trusted team members to whom we can delegate data analysis, modeling, budgeting, or business case development. There are consulting firms that will make recommendations on what to do over the next few years. All such things have their place. But the one thing we cannot really outsource as leaders is the need to *think strategically*. We must demonstrate that ourselves. Why?

1. Our people look to *us* for clarity. They want to know what *we* think. They're trusting us to sift through all the competing ideas and priorities to arrive at well-considered decisions that best serve the shared purpose and interests. To do that we need original thinking of our own to sense-check all the other opinions and options vying for attention. This includes the ability to see the whole and see further ahead. To recognize the traps of conventional wisdom and side-step them;

2. While we see what everyone else sees, we need to think what no one else has thought. Otherwise, we remain bunched up in the pack, unable to break through or to create new value. If we're to step forward into new territory, we need the courage of both our convictions and our comprehension. That requires us to develop greater insight and foresight than that available in the public domain.

3. We must be able to explain the direction and its logic to our own team or to consultants. If we haven't framed the problem or opportunity thoughtfully ourselves, we get whatever others decide it is. Their frame becomes the de facto view, taking on a life of its own. A year or two later we may realize we've been barking up the wrong tree, having wasted a lot of time and resource in the process. As leaders we need to invest in the up-front thinking that sets our planning and implementation processes on the right course from the outset.

> *"Vision is unavailable to those*
> *who cannot see with their own eyes."*
>
> —Henry Mintzberg

As a first step we need to draw the less familiar craft of strategic *thinking* out from the more common activities of strategic *planning*. These are related disciplines but are best understood distinctly. In practice many people conflate the two or slip straight into planning mode without adequate exploration or forethought. To do so is to risk missing the forest for the trees.

We *think* first, *plan* later.

What is strategic thinking? In the academic literature there are a variety of definitions, but they can be somewhat convoluted. For our purposes we need something more instructive. Something we can easily carry in our minds and apply whenever needed (which is often). It is simply ***the ability to identify—and think through—the set of choices most pivotal to the realization of our purpose***. Let's break this down:

"the ability"	Strategic thinking is more a mindset or skill, than an annual event or formal document.
"to identify"	Recognizing what really matters amongst all the complexitites and pressures of our environments. Determining which questions to ask can be just as difficult as determining the answers themselves.
"and think through"	Purposefully gathering relevant insights and ideas from all available sources, exploring the options, and playing out the possible implications in our minds.
"the set of choices most pivotal"	Strategy is fundamentally about choices. Usually there are several particularly important ones to make. Some are so consequential that the alternative answers could send us in very different directions. Our decision on any one of these will profoundly affect others. Hence, they need to cohere and reinforce one another. Ideally, we should focus on the smallest set of choices that will collectively make the greatest difference.
"to the realization of our purpose"	Purpose is the reason behind our reasoning. It defines success. It is the one sure and stable element amongst many variables. It serves as a touchstone against which we might assess the potential fit of each option. It is the narrative thread that runs through our key choices, helping tie everything together.

Strategic planning tends to be a periodic effort in which goals are translated into a series of actions and resource allocations. It generally happens at retreats or workshops and sometimes by engaging an external consultancy firm. While *strategic planning* is a misnomer because strategy and planning have different foci and require different thought processes, the reality is that the term lives on in many organizations. In practice our teams need some basis on which they can capture the organization's priorities, initiate action, and measure progress. They need some reference point for their forecasts, budgets, and the like. Boards and other key stakeholders need some tangible assurance that we've thought ahead and are suitably prepared. This often takes the form of a document labeled as a strategic plan, business plan, or something similar.

A manager needs excellent planning skills. A leader needs to be a strategic thinker.

Strategy is about *formulating* our key choices. Planning is about preparing to *activate* them. The intent here is not to pit one against the other, for they are complementary. Nor is it to discount the value of planning per se. Rather it is to bring strategic thinking to the fore, identifying it as the essential, higher-order discipline of an effective leader. A strong strategic thinker can be more aware, agile, and creative *and* develop more insightful business plans. But it's unlikely to flow the other way if our thinking starts with a template at the commencement of the annual planning cycle.

If we don't first explore the wider landscape, how can we be sure that we're playing the right game or setting the right priorities? If we're focusing mostly within our own enterprise, how can we have any confidence that we won't be blindsided? If we're simply adding five percent to last year's income targets, how can we have any confidence that the market will comply with what our spreadsheets say? If we don't possess meaningful points of difference, how do we know they'll come to us at all? If we plan only on the basis of what we already know and are familiar with, how can we expect to achieve any more than small increments? We might even go backwards if we're just treading water when the flow is against us. There will come times when merely tweaking our plans will not be enough to sustain progress. Hence, planning cannot become a substitute for strategy, nor should the two be confused.

"Strategy doesn't come from a calendar-driven process; it isn't the product of a systematic search for ways of earning above average profits; strategy comes from viewing the world in... new and unconventional ways."

—Gary Hamel

There's value in taking a closer look at the differences. Strategic thinking has several distinctives, but three of these are particularly important to understand first:

1. Strategic choices are of a **higher order**.
2. Those choices are **interrelated** and so should be considered together.
3. Our mental radar around strategic issues should be **always on**.

Higher Order

The word *strategic* is thrown around a lot, so let's be clear on what we mean by it in this context. *Strategic* means "highly important to or an integral part of a strategy." It is most properly applied to larger aims or to matters affecting overall success (such as winning a war, serving our purpose, strengthening the enterprise as a whole). It speaks of those choices that have heightened value because the ends we seek cannot be realized without getting them right. But if we do, they put us in a position from which real impact and growth becomes possible.

In the diagram below *purpose* sits at the top of the tree. If we are genuinely purpose-driven, this is its natural place in the hierarchy. It is the reason we are here, the end we have in mind, and a guide for all our key decisions in between.

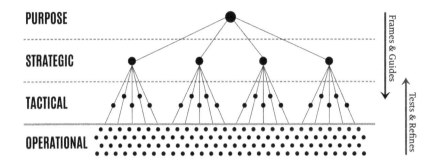

> *"You must make strategy the servant rather than the master.*
> *Strategies are time-bound and target specific results.*
> *Your purpose, in contrast, is what makes you durably relevant*
> *to the world. Strategy is but one of several important means to*
> *operationalize your purpose. Intrinsic human connection*
> *to your purpose is even more important."[1]*

The strategic layer is a relatively small set of key choices that align and mobilize our organization toward the realization of its purpose. They might be thought of as the proverbial 20 percent of choices that collectively make 80 percent of the difference to our prospects of sustained success. For example, some strategic questions are:

- Who are we here to serve?
- What is the real problem to be solved?
- What's our highest, and most unique, contribution to that end?
- How might that solution scale in order to help more people?
- What capabilities will we need to excel at if we're to deliver that?

Such questions go to the heart of what it takes to grow income and have an impact. Any one of these decisions profoundly affects everything that follows. Hence, they are of a higher order of importance. Of course, smart tactical moves and operational excellence are also vitally important. But true success is conditional upon having first made the right strategic choices. Great execution in the wrong direction is of little value. We must ensure we're doing the right things first, *then* focus on doing them right.

Strategic thinking is also of a higher order in that it calls for a more insightful and nuanced understanding of what's going on externally and internally. It's not as simple as merely observing trends, accepting opinions as given, or running numbers through a model. Rather, we recognize that we often don't know the whole story and so there's a need to explore more widely, and dig deeper, if we're to make good decisions. To do so we need to be more authentically engaged with both the topic and the people. We need to be more interested in context and more attuned to the needs. We must be more curious, being prepared to ask questions others are not. We need to be better able to unravel complexity and understand why things are the way they are and be able to sense shifts, see patterns, and make new connections. We need to be able to anticipate what might happen under different scenarios and to solve problems and design new solutions.

The quality of outcome depends on the quality of our thinking in these respects.

Interrelated

In practice strategic choices are rarely as linear as they might be in planning, or as siloed as in the figure above. The decision we make on one factor will typically have implications for others. They need to work together. Hence, they are best considered as an integrated set of choices. One in which they are mutually reinforcing and in which the whole becomes more than just the sum of its parts.

It's not feasible to think through all the relationships between the hundreds of detailed decisions we might have to make over the year(s) ahead. But it *is* possible to do that for the smaller number of higher-level choices that 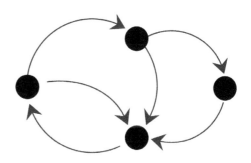 form the core of our strategy (and from which most other tactical and operational decisions spring). If these strategic choices flow together cohesively, there's a good chance that our activation will as well. This requires that we develop more of a systems-level view of our space and understand how greater impact and value could be created.

The interrelated nature of these choices means that we take an iterative approach in answering and aligning them. On our first pass we might form an initial view or hypothesis of what the best option might be, but hold loosely to that until we've also considered the other related elements. We need to test both the merits of each choice and their fit with one another. If one of our options is not the best available, or is not meshing well, we rethink it. Often this process is repeated many times before building sufficient confidence that we're on the right track and that a sound strategy is starting to take shape.

Like the chef seeking to create a new signature dish, this can involve some messiness as we experiment with different ingredients and combinations. It can seem that a lot of our early work gets scrapped, but it's all an essential part of the creative process. The mastery of our craft is evident in both what ends up on the plate *and* what gets put in the bin. It's much about choices of what we're not going to do as what we will.

In strategy, as in cuisine, less can be more—especially when a few quality ingredients come together in a new and harmonic way.

Always On

When do we need to be thinking strategically? *Constantly.* Not in any kind of anxiety-ridden or hypervigilant way, but simply by remaining aware of what's going on and being mindful of potential implications.

Business planning tends to be a cyclical event, so we normally focus on it at a certain time of year, such as in the lead up to preparing next year's budget. In contrast, strategic thinking is required whenever there are new developments, which is to say just about every day.

We need to assess the potential impact of any such shift. Does our strategy still stack up? Do we need to fine tune our approach? Does it open a new opportunity? How might we use the change or innovation or insight to our advantage? This requires some kind of mental receiver capable of picking up and processing such signals. In practice, however, leaders tend to be time poor, often consumed with operational matters. It's a common lament:

> *In one survey of 10,000 senior leaders, 97 percent of them said that being strategic was the leadership behavior most important to their organization's success. And yet in another study, a full 96 percent of the leaders surveyed said they lacked the time for strategic thinking.*[2]

This being the case, we have three options. First, we can intentionally carve out more time for strategic thinking. That is well worth doing to the extent possible. But given the other demands on our time it may never seem enough. Second, we can keep our strategy as simple and clear as possible, choosing not to sweat the small stuff, so it takes less time to assess every new development. That too is worthwhile, so long as we make it as simple as it can be, without being too simplistic. Finally, we can develop the ability to detect potentially relevant signals, make a mental note, then assess them more fully when we have time. Let's focus in on that idea.

By way of analogy, think of a fighter jet equipped with both active and passive radar. The active radar sends out a pulse, listening for a return signal to proactively identify other objects in its environment. An active radar can search at a longer range, detect more objects, and provide richer data, but it's used only selectively as it can also give away the fighter's position to an adversary. A passive radar, on the other hand, only receives signals from other objects that are transmitting. It is activated more consistently as there is a lower risk of detection by the enemy. It doesn't pick up on everything, but it's still a very useful capability, enhancing the pilot's situational awareness even when they are focused on other tasks.

Put another way, active radar is like a powerful searchlight, whereas passive radar is more akin to a low-energy motion sensor—perhaps not as far-reaching but still sufficient to alert us to movements that may warrant a closer look.

In terms of strategic thinking our passive radar is simply asking ourselves how each new development relates to our purpose and how it affects our key strategic choices—quickly running it through those filters. Oftentimes the answer may be very little or not at all. Or it might simply be confirmation we're on the right track. But when there's an incongruence, our mental red light will flash, alerting us of the need to investigate.

Either way strategic thinking is constantly required. Before we start planning, after we've implemented the plan and reflected on what we've learned, and at every stage in between as we assess and respond to the unfolding circumstances. This becomes second nature and even part of the joy of our work—if we weave it into the everyday rhythm of leadership.

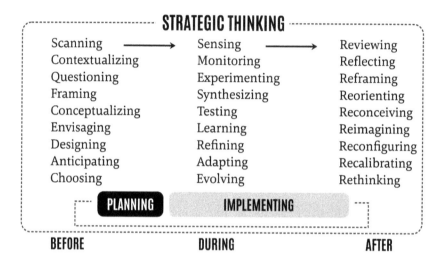

The higher-order, inter-related, and always-on nature of strategic thinking gives rise to several other ways in which it differs from a planning mindset. In particular, our relationship with:

- **intent** (whether we're aiming at a fixed target, or more dynamic outcomes)
- **time** (the timeframe we have in mind as we consider the way forward)
- **detail** (the level of abstraction or ambiguity we can work with)
- **insight** (what we consider as worthy inputs into our thinking)
- **possibilities** (what future options we can see and are prepared to entertain)

- **resources** (our view of what we might be able to access or leverage)
- **action** (whether thinking and doing are seen as sequential or interactive)

In various ways we'll pick up on these characteristics in the chapters that follow, progressively adding them to our strategic thinking repertoire.

A Prepared Mind

"The mind can only see what it is prepared to see."

—Edward de Bono

There's nothing mysterious about strategic thinking. Conceptually it's simpler than many might suppose. It's focusing on a specific purpose to serve, not trying to change the world by ourselves. Strategic thinking considers a few key choices not hundreds. It's thinking about the best direction not trying to precisely predict the future. It is, as described earlier, the ability to identify and think through the set of choices most pivotal to the realization of our purpose.

Simple right? In the abstract, yes. But it's not so easy in practice—largely because our own heads get in the way. We struggle to see differently because we've inadvertently locked ourselves into a familiar perspective or set of assumptions. Even when we do try to be more expansive in our thinking, we may find ourselves being drawn back in by the gravitational pull of old habits, preconceived ideas, or the conventional views of those around us. In addition, we don't know what we don't know in part because we might not yet have asked the right questions or considered other viewpoints or taken time to explore new spaces.

This difficulty is compounded by the distraction of all the other urgent matters competing for our attention. But we must find a way. There's an old retort from Hollywood directors to producers pressuring them for a speedy conclusion to filming, so they could save cost and begin monetizing the product. "Do you want it fast or good?" the directors would say. The same principle often applies to matters of strategy. If you want it fast just go with your gut or hold a workshop or imitate another organization or download a planning template and fill in the boxes. But if you want a good strategy, you have to think intentionally, laterally, and holistically—and that takes time. It requires metacognition: that we *think about our thinking* and consciously adopt an approach suited to the task at hand.

Finding new headspace requires taking off one mindset and putting on another, almost as though it were a hat. Putting on a new thinking cap as it were. Just as we select our clothes in the morning based on our activities and anticipated conditions for that day, so too we must intentionally choose and "put on" the thinking approach that will best suit our purposes when contemplating issues of strategic importance.

This is not as foreign as it might seem at first. We do it in everyday life, such as when we switch between being a parent at home and a professional at work. We're still the same person but our mind naturally shifts from one mode to another because that's what the situation requires.

Say you're a footballer with your position always having been in defense. One day, mid-way through the game, you're asked to move into the offense for the first time. Even though you've been playing with the team and know the plays, a mental reorientation is required. You have to look at the field differently, reconceive what an opportunity looks like, look for different kinds of signals, lead differently. For example, you'd seek to break away from your opponent, rather than stick to them like glue.

Now imagine you'd just been appointed coach. Another, even bigger, shift in thinking would be required. You'd still be interested in how the individual plays unfold, but now you'd be looking for patterns, learning from them so that those insights could be utilized in future. Your view would zoom out to think about the game as a whole. You might play out different options in your mind about what plays to call. Afterward you may reflect on what you'd observed to determine what should be done differently next game, or even next season. You'd identify the core skills the team needs to improve or how the team culture might need to evolve if they're to be successful in future. You'd wrap those thoughts up into a cohesive narrative so that the overall picture that's in your mind could be communicated back to the team.

A chief executive might spend much of their day in a management mindset. But when it's time to meet with the board of directors or a group of potential investors, a reorientation is required. Most of the operational detail temporarily fades into the background to allow more strategic matters to come to the fore. The agenda is important, the stakes are high, and everyone's time is at a premium. So, the conversation rightly focuses on the critical issues most likely to affect the future trajectory and health of the business.

What happens if we need fresh strategic thinking but still have our operational hat on? We'd likely experience only incremental improvements on what we're already doing. If we still had our accounting hat on, our strategy would probably look more like a financial model, focusing on where we can eke out more margin. If we had our risk management hat on, we might recommend a more defensive approach. Instead, we must thoughtfully put on the mindset that reflects the kind of strategy we want to see. We'll go back to being a CFO or member of the risk committee later. There is a time and place for fiduciary oversight and risk analysis, but when strategy is called for, those details need to temporarily take a back seat while we consider higher-order issues.

A prepared mind in this regard is one that is

- willing to really go after the purpose the organization stands for.
- willing to step outside our usual frame of reference and explore more broadly.
- willing to question the orthodoxies of how the business or sector works today.
- willing to inject insight and inspiration from sources outside the norm.
- willing to stand in others' shoes and consider another perspective.
- willing to entertain different scenarios in our minds, looking for new ways through.
- willing to iterate until the whole is as strong and impactful as it can be.

I repeat the word *willing* here to reinforce the notion that it requires a conscious decision to temporarily put aside our usual way of thinking in favor of one that is a better fit for the task at hand. That may be a stretch at first, but you'll become more adept in time. Strategic thinking is a skill that like any other is developed through practice.

We know we're on the right track when we begin to see, in our mind's eye, the outlines of a better future. We are moving in the right direction when we perceive things in their wider context, pick up on cues we'd previously missed, discern what resides at the heart of the matter, detect new openings, and imagine how things could come together differently. Our mind sees only what it's prepared to see. It is our lens on the world, framing what is before us and bringing the most important elements into focus.

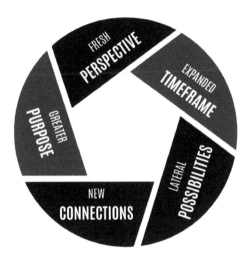

So how might we open our minds to see more strategically? Our mind is like the aperture of a camera. The aperture is the opening in the lens through which more or less light is admitted into the picture. The larger the aperture the more light is allowed in, resulting in a brighter image. Hence, it's often used in low-light situations. In strategic thinking—especially in situations where the future seems somewhat fuzzy or dim—we similarly need to open our minds, letting in more "light" to help us make out the key features in the picture before us.

The downside of a larger aperture is that it reduces the depth of field, so some of the finer details in the background may be less clear. But for the purposes of strategic thinking this is often a necessary trade off. It's usually more important that we first get our heads around the context and bring the key subjects into focus. We'll be able to address more specific questions later, and test and refine our thinking as we move forward.

In my experience there's five key ways of widening our perspective to allow more strategically useful information to come into view.

1. **Think Big:** Perceive through the lens of a greater purpose
2. **Think Outside the Box:** Seek fresh perspectives
3. **Think Ahead:** Expand the timeframe
4. **Think Again:** Explore lateral possibilities
5. **Think Through:** Find new connections

Think Big

Purpose is primary for all the reasons described earlier. It frames, focuses, and illuminates all that follows. We don't know *what* to look for until we know *why* we're looking. If we're not scanning the situation with a clear intent, we'll simply be staring at the same monochrome picture that had us scratching our heads in the first place. But looking through the lens of our purpose we begin to see possibilities and nuances that might otherwise have been overlooked, and in more vivid color as it were. It's like putting on opportunity goggles.

Purpose helps us make sense of what is going on by situating elements within a bigger story. It is essential for identifying what matters most. Strategy is a high-context sport. We understand our circumstances better when we first comprehend the wider forces and conditions in operation around us.

If we think of strategy as being only a series of targets to be pursued one after another, we get a narrower and more linear view of the world. We take small steps from the certainty of the present toward a nearer-term, directly observable objective. An approach that focuses on series of sequential steps like this is more of a planning mindset—strategy by default rather than a bolder and more intentional strategy by design.

In contrast if we start with a clear purpose, our eyes are lifted, tending to go to the bigger picture first, taking in more of the landscape and the range of possibilities within it. We see and choose the end from the beginning and scan for alternative ways of getting there.

The two forms of thinking run in opposite directions. The kind of target-based process used in planning runs present-forward. Purpose-based thinking is often more future-back in nature. Both are useful at the right time. But in matters of strategy, it is generally better to start with the end in mind, and with an outlook that lets in more contextual information.

Another difference is that with a planning mindset we tend to place ourselves at the center of the picture, with our principal concern being our next steps. It's like walking down a road on a pitch-black night carrying only a torch. That's very helpful for illuminating what's right in front of you, the next pothole, but less instructive when it comes to the direction ahead. In contrast, a purpose-driven approach is more like a light on a hill. It sets our eyes on the prize, and those we serve, rather than on ourselves. In this way we are more oriented toward the end game and may be more attuned to signals from the environment around us. We develop a clearer sense of direction and can begin to make out some outline of the way ahead, even if only faint.

Purpose is the beacon. Strategy is finding the best route to get there. Planning is about the incremental steps along that path. They're all important but the order matters. Purpose comes first.

Think Outside the Box

To think outside the box is to get outside our own limited field of vision and see things from a fresh perspective. It is to think unconventionally so that we might uncover some new insight, idea or opening.

Even one such external viewpoint is an advance. But it's much better if we can integrate multiple perspectives, building more of a 3D understanding of the challenges and opportunities. Building on this metaphor we might say that we are mentally…

- *Helicoptering* up and down to better comprehend the situation as a whole—whether that's a ten-thousand-foot view or hovering close to the action. The combination of the two allows us to understand what's going on at both a macro and micro level.
- *Walking around* the problem, appreciating the different facets or dimensions of the situation, and interpreting it from other perspectives.
- *Zooming in and out* like a photographer in order to get just the right amount of information in the frame.

Such metaphors remind us of the need to view our situation at different levels of abstraction and from different angles, enabling us to have a more holistic understanding of the issues and their context. We pick up on nuances we might not otherwise have seen. We become more assured that we are coming at it from a helpful angle. The problems begin to seem smaller. Our minds and our choices become clearer.

"A change in perspective is worth 80 IQ points."

—Alan Kay

The key is in *empathy* and *perspective-taking*—thinking about a situation from another point-of-view. We transport ourselves outside our own minds into those of others, imagining what they might see, experience, think, feel, or believe about the matter. In effect we're decentralizing our view—recognizing that we're not the center of the universe or the fount of all wisdom—and that others may have a valid perspective. We don't have to agree with those views, but it is always useful to understand them.

Who we consult and empathize with is a particularly important question. Almost always the views of customers (or others we exist to serve) will be primary. Staff and board members are also rich sources of insight—and key stakeholders in the strategy process. Beyond that there may be others such as government, suppliers, partners, funders, and the like, depending on what is most relevant in the situation.

In cases where we need fresher views, we may need to cast our net wider, bringing some additional and unconventional perspectives into the mix. Innovators on the fringe. Lessons from other sectors. Our critics perhaps. We might explore ideas as to how we'd gain an advantage over our enterprise if we were a competitor. We might imagine what we'd do if some other thought leader or entrepreneur were sitting in our seat. (More on this in the section entitled "Develop Holographic Insight.")

Think Ahead

Purpose, strategy, and leadership are all activities principally concerned with success in the long run. Exemplars of each demonstrate foresight and take a principled approach. They'll resist today's pressure to take the more expedient path when they know there's a better way, one likely to realize greater social and economic prosperity tomorrow. They think and lead with an expanded timeframe in mind.

And yet short-termism is everywhere. We see it in political cycles, in listed companies scrambling to meet stock market expectations, and perhaps in our own organization. It arises from a desire to placate one stakeholder or another, to get some monkey off our back, to conceal a deficiency, or to avoid having to make hard choices or stretch beyond our comfort zone. But in the final analysis making decisions that will benefit only in the near term is borrowing from tomorrow to pay today. A strategic approach runs in the opposite direction. It understands that the future starts today and that the courage and consistency we exhibit now will pay greater dividends in the end.

Both scenarios involve a cost, a return, and a compounding effect over time. If we invest in doing the right thing now, it's the advantages that will accumulate over time. If we take the short-term gain now, it's the adverse impacts or lost opportunities that will mount up.

"Today I will do what others won't,
so tomorrow I can accomplish what others can't."

—Jerry Rice

If we take the long view and lead resolutely in that direction, a number of benefits may accrue. We waste less on detours and U-turns and instead invest in the things that matter more in the long run. We build a deeper form of credibility and confidence. And we get into prime position earlier, creating the possibility of first-leader advantage. This is not to say we might not have to zig-zag on occasion, but we can still do this without taking our eyes off the prize, always purposefully working our way toward the goal, even if somewhat diagonally at times.

So how do we do that in practice? How might we transcend short-termism? How can we strike the right balance between dealing with present demands and future drivers of success? By expanding our mental time frame to include the future, the present, and the past at once. In this way we can situate our decisions within a bigger story and be more conscious of their likely ripple effects. This has also been described as "thinking in time."[3]

Perhaps the best way to understand this is to break it down into a series of short statements:

Strategy is essentially about a direction to head in, so as to reach an intended destination (i.e., the future).

Progress toward our strategic goals requires thoughtful (and sometimes, courageous) choices today (i.e., in the present).

Those choices will be informed in part by the purpose for which our enterprise was created; where we have come from; what we have learned; and the culture, capabilities, and connections we possess as a result (i.e., products of the past).

If we can align all three within a cohesive narrative, we have an expanded sense of time, a long arc within which today's pressures may seem a little smaller, having been placed in their wider context. We get a sense of constructive continuity from the past, general direction for the future, and a greater calmness and clarity in the present. Today's priorities and decisions should, to the maximum extent possible, build *on* the past and build *for* the desired future.

If any one of these past-present-future coordinates is missing, we run the risk of "losing the plot," slipping back into short-termism. But if we keep moving forward with this expanded timeframe in view, we're better able to make genuinely strategic choices.

Having a long view still leaves the challenge of stretching beyond the familiar as we look further ahead. One way to extend our comfort zone is to think of time in distinct horizons, giving ourselves permission to be more exploratory and creative in the outer zones. We don't have to be Nostradamus, trying to predict future events, but we can at least be clear on our intent and general direction. And we can think through the possibilities and scenarios.

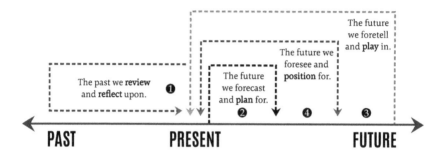

Each of the time horizons illustrated above requires a somewhat different way of thinking, but collectively they build a much richer and longer-range picture than any one perspective can alone. Again, let's break this down.

1. **Review and reflect upon the past.** When we review and reflect upon the past, we look through the lens of our purpose and in the light of what we want to achieve in future. What have we learned that will be useful in future? What capabilities and assets have we developed that can be leveraged going forward? What should we leave behind? *This thinking runs from the present to the past.*

2. **Future we forecast and plan for.** The future we can already see will likely be relatively short term. Perhaps a year or so ahead (though probably less in more dynamic environments. This depends more on one's context than any rule of thumb we might

posit here). Whatever the case, it makes sense to plan for that which can be reliably planned for—no longer and no less. You'll need to be the judge of what that time frame is. *This thinking runs from the present to the future.*

3. **Future we foretell and play in.** Way off in the horizon is a tomorrow that has not yet been fully determined. To a greater or lesser extent, it's still up for grabs and belongs to those who would boldly shape it. This is the future we foretell and play in. It's not about clairvoyance or wishful thinking but rather about visioning and innovation. It's as though we're standing in tomorrow, looking around, imagining what a better future could look like and how that might be brought about. We bring those ideas back into today as options to factor into today's strategic choices. We may even begin experimenting and investing now toward that end. *This thinking runs from the future back to the present.*

4. **Future we foresee and position for.** In the mid-range is the future we foresee and position for. We determine its nature and shape through a combination of *projecting forward* from what we know or can reasonably anticipate and *working backwards* from the future we're aiming for. Somewhere in the creative tension between those two thought directions (insight and foresight) is a *position* we believe we should and could occupy. One that's necessary to bring about the desired future and which we assess as being possible given where we're coming from. In this place we accept that we're operating with incomplete information and that there are no guarantees. Nevertheless, we can still come up with a reasoned view of what an ideal position would be. Metaphorically speaking, this is the high ground or hill we need

to take in the battle in order to put ourselves in a place from which we can subsequently win the war. It is a function of both what we believe can be achieved between now and then, and what it is that we want to realize on the other side. Hence *this thinking reconciles the future-to-present and present-to-future views.*

All of this requires accepting some degree of ambiguity and uncertainty, after obtaining all the supporting knowledge we reasonably can. This works in practice so long as it's matched with a preparedness to refine, adapt, or revisit our thinking as the future unfolds.

If we link these horizons together in one picture, we have our expanded time frame. The beginnings of a narrative or roadmap connecting past, present and future.

Think Again

It stands to reason that strategic innovation is more likely to come from considering a wider range of possibilities than a narrower set. To think again is to ensure we explore all the possibilities. Creativity is more likely to be sparked by entertaining insights and inspirations from outside the norm. Imaginative exploration may not be a great idea when conducting brain surgery, but it is when seeking new answers to seemingly intractable social or economic problems. Indeed, how many of today's advances began with an audacious, left-field vision that challenged the status quo? Think Intel, Tesla, Apple, CNN, Uber, FedEx and the like.

Any view that imagination is inherently inferior to logical reasoning serves only to limit the possibility of a breakthrough. Logic is about connecting validated facts and this is clearly very important. But to rely on that alone is to limit ourselves to only what is already known. Imagination on the other hand has no such boundaries. It is the curiosity needed to discover or develop something new. If we're trying to expand our thinking and develop new answers, it must be part of the mix. How much more powerful it is to combine both ideas *and* evidence, creativity *and* logic, exploration *and* analysis in their right measure. To regain balance some of us need to give ourselves permission to dream and play more, being assured that this is a legitimate and necessary part of strategic thinking.

The point is illustrated in the concept of divergent and convergent thinking, a term coined by American psychologist Joy Paul Guilford in the 1950s.

By pushing outside the familiar, we develop lateral thoughts and perspectives that might not otherwise have occurred to us. We expand our possibilities by thinking more broadly first.

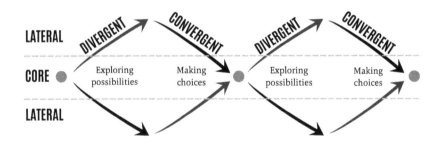

Divergent thinking looks for every conceivable way in which we could address the challenge before us. Ideally, we want a wide range of options that, collectively, are as close to exhaustive as we can get (even if some are really "out there"). Once we have that we can then switch to convergent thinking mode, working our way through the options to find those that best fit our purpose, need, and context. That is, turn our long list into a short list, and ultimately, into the best available choice.

Though it may feel like a mental roller coaster at times, it's far better to work in this kind of disciplined rhythm than to limit our options too quickly, or worse, not even be willing to explore. The payoff is that we are more likely to find new angles, fresh ideas, and differentiated positions. Sometimes the most lateral insight, from what at first seems the most unlikely source, is the one that cracks the case.

> *"The need to be right all the time is the biggest bar to new ideas.*
> *It is better to have enough ideas for some of them to be wrong*
> *than to be always right by having no ideas at all."*
>
> —Edward de Bono

A similar principle applies to the resources we believe could be available to us. Often, we might dismiss an opportunity as being beyond us because we don't control those levers. We're low on capital, on time, on knowledge, on influence, or whatever. Accordingly, we shut down some lines of inquiry, not even thinking them a possibility, and set our sights a little lower.

But it's often the most constrained change agents who end up having the greatest impact, demonstrating that an apparent lack of resource need not stand in the way. Consider the grieving parents, or the victim of an injustice, whose passionate advocacy sparks a social movement. Consider the ingenuity of the farmer or entrepreneur who invents clever low-cost solutions using only what they have at hand. The penniless migrants or refugees who create booming businesses from scratch. The start-ups acquired by larger firms because they've managed to innovate something the larger, cash-rich company was not able to.

Such (social or business) entrepreneurship has been famously defined as, "the pursuit of opportunity beyond resources controlled" by Howard Stevenson, the godfather of entrepreneurship studies at Harvard Business School.[4] The proponent's resources might be relatively meagre, perhaps limited to intangibles such as a vision of what could be, a talent, some street smarts, and a determination to make it happen. The other assets needed to bring that vision to fruition—money, technology, distribution networks, political connections, and the like—may be held by others. But direct control of those elements needn't be the deciding factor for they can sometimes be accessed through other means, such as through partnerships, social networks, grants, or investors. Where there's a will there's a way.

If our view of resource availability shifts, so too do the possibilities. Those who take a strength-based view see the potential to leverage abilities or assets they already possess, even if only very modest. Those with an abundance mindset see opportunities everywhere—to contribute, to learn, to align, to partner. Those who understand themselves to be part of an ecosystem can collaborate with others. They seek not only to *get* for themselves but also to *give,* to be of value to others in a mutually beneficial relationship. In each case we're both better appreciating what we have and taking a wider account of other resources around us that perhaps could be co-opted in some way.

> *"Abundance is not a result you create.*
> *It is an existing state you recognize."*
>
> —Ralph Waldo Emerson

One final point: If we want to expand our possibilities, we also need to re-examine our relationship with risk. Just about every strategic choice involves some level of uncertainty or potential downside. So, if we're overly risk averse and discard options too early in our thought process, our view of available possibilities narrows too quickly. That's not to say we should embrace fanciful ideas or throw caution to the wind. Rather, it is to see risk as being an important but secondary consideration, something to be managed instead of avoided altogether.

Opportunity and risk come as a set. Without risk there can be no growth, no impact, and no testing of what may be possible. A farmer assumes risk when they plant their seed, but this is in the context of an anticipated harvest. If they held back from sowing for fear of drought, they'd never reap anything. Ditto for the investor, the entrepreneur, the social change agent, the citizen running for public office.

Correctly ordering our thinking helps ensure we're not self-sabotaging our own prospects. We put the first thing first (opportunity) and then consider its potential pitfalls (risks). The expansive "what if" (or divergent) view first followed by more sober "if then" (or convergent) thinking to qualify and focus our options. We *take* the opportunity; we *manage* the risk.

> *"It's not because things are difficult that we dare not venture. It's*
> *because we dare not venture that they are difficult."*
> —Seneca

Risk itself need not be prohibitory. It's merely something we factor into our strategy. For example, we might seek expert advice to test our thinking, take a route that lessens the probability or severity of a risk's occurrence, pace our approach so we're not biting off too much at once, factor contingencies into our budget, or share the risk with others.

Naturally we should decline paths that could put us into an unrecoverable position, betting the farm as it were. We always want to have some options up our sleeve and leave room to pivot from a call that doesn't work out.

If we remain opportunity focused, preserve optionality, and manage foreseeable risks sensibly, we can keep moving forward. Of course, unanticipated obstacles will pop up along the way, but we negotiate these as they emerge. Indeed, that is often the only point at which they can be identified and managed. In those situations, the choice is a pragmatic one: we either find a way or make one.

Think Through

Every choice has consequences. Those consequences can be either direct or indirect, intended or unintended. The original Latin *consequentia* means "to follow after." That is exactly what we're seeking to anticipate: what comes after we take one action or another. The operative question here is, What would happen if….?

Given that strategy involves an interrelated set of choices, and because we typically operate in some kind of community and ecosystem, any one decision will usually also affect others. To think through is to find those connections. Hence, we must identify the causal or reinforcing relationships in the situation before us and consider the likely ripple effects of what we might choose to do. Ideally, we want to set off a virtuous sequence of events not a vicious cycle that comes back to bite us or those we serve.

In the first instance we assess our options on their own merits and form an early view of what we think might be the most beneficial decision. This is about the direct impact of that choice. But, once again, it's best to hold lightly to that until we've also considered two other kinds of consequences: trade-offs and knock-on effects.

A **trade-off** arises in a zero-sum situation where taking one path necessarily means losing the potential opportunities and benefits of taking another. For example, if we turn right at an intersection, we've passed up that opportunity to go left. In a business setting it's usually difficult to be both the lowest-cost provider and the one providing the highest level of service or customization. So we chose one as our preferred strategic position understanding that it may leave the other position open to others. Hence, we think through the implications to assess the likely trade-offs of each option. At these junctures we ask ourselves what we are prepared to forego or risk in order to gain the benefits of the alternative.

A **knock-on effect** is when an action or decision has indirect or cumulative implications. We might also think of this as a domino effect. Once the first domino in a sequence is knocked over, it has consequences for the second, the third, and any others in that line. Often that's about avoiding a potentially detrimental outcome. Having thought the matter through, we realize that a certain choice may ultimately do more harm than good or have some other unintended result, and so we look for other ways forward.

Say we have the option of taking on a big new program funded by a government grant. It may look like a great opportunity to extend our social impact, but there are downsides. It increases our reliance on a single source of income, meaning we become more beholden to the one funder. It also comes with a range of conditions that will likely constrain our freedom to operate as we wish in some areas. It involves a high compliance burden, increasing our cost. This may also have the effect of limiting our ability to innovate or adapt our service. In turn this risks the culture of empowerment and innovation we've been cultivating for years, turning our organization into more of a program-oriented rather than customer-oriented provider. Such are the knock-on effects of that initial decision to take on the grant.

Conversely, within this same scenario there might also be an opportunity to trigger a chain reaction that works in our favor. For example, it might give us scale efficiencies or access to new capital or service points or information that could be used to great advantage. Either way it's hard to put the toothpaste back in the tube, so to speak, once we've acted, so it's important that we play out these scenarios (knock-on effects) in our mind beforehand, and anticipate the likely implications of any such move, before we make a final decision.

Thinking through is essentially developing an end-to-end view of how value and impact is created in our space and anticipating how that might be either improved or inhibited by taking the option before us. The answer could be anywhere from some modest incremental change to a major shift that (positively or negatively) disrupts the way things are done. Amazon and Apple are commonly cited examples. Both companies created new value by cutting out the middleman and inserting themselves into the picture with a new model and proposition.

"Creativity is just connecting things."
—Steve Jobs

To do this we need to think relationally about how the pieces could come together in new and better ways. This is an iterative process of mentally pulling those pieces apart and reassembling them in different configurations. We need to think about what we might keep, remove, inject, combine, or re-order to create greater value and impact. One or more scenarios might strike us as holding real promise, thereby creating another strategic option to consider.

The idea is to focus our attention on those few factors that hold greatest sway over the desired outcome. It's important to get to the heart of the matter and play around with those variables. Doing so helps identify the smallest number of moves we could make that would collectively make the greatest difference. Or to be even sharper, we might ask ourselves "what's the *one thing* we could do that'd change the game altogether?" This focused way of thinking tends to generate richer ideas. Even if we don't find a silver bullet answer, we at least have stretched ourselves to identify the best options available in the circumstances. It's also good to know where our limits are—where our role ends and the rest of the ecosystem begins. Where we can do it ourselves and where we need to partner with others. We find new connections and combinations and avoid unintended consequences by analyzing the implications of alternative courses of actions. Doing so helps us to recognize we are not an island and that if we are to succeed, we must think and act systemically.

Metaphorically Speaking

"A good sketch is better than a long speech."
—Napoleon Bonaparte

We now have both clear purpose and a mindset attuned to strategic possibilities. It's an exciting combination. The next step is to simplify and sequence the choices therein.

In the rest of this section we'll build a framework on the foundation now established. One that may help you find clarity in your own circumstances. By framework I mean a set of principles that leaves plenty of room for the application of your own expertise, creativity, and judgment. This contrasts with a methodology or tool, like a balanced scorecard or a business model canvas, which tend to be more task specific. These certainly have their place, so long as we're clear on when they're the right tool for the job. They must remain an aid to strategic thinking and not become a substitute for it. Draw upon these as you see fit, but for our purposes we'll focus more on the higher-level scaffolding that gives structure and cohesion to our thinking.

Here we reintroduce the "fog" metaphor, representing the ambiguity or uncertainty of the strategic situation before us, and through which we must find some kind of clarity.

As you may have noticed, throughout this book I've used a range of metaphors, analogies, anecdotes, simple whiteboard-style graphics, quotations, and stories from other spaces in an attempt to explain complex concepts more simply. (Referred to collectively as "metaphors" henceforth for ease of reference). A resonant metaphor is often worth a  thousand words. They create a mental picture that helps us connect a new concept to something we're already familiar with or can easily imagine. They help us see things in a new light and see into the heart of the matter. Metaphors may also be useful to you in conveying strategic ideas more succinctly and vividly to your own staff and stakeholders. A strategy is of limited value if it doesn't capture the imagination and isn't widely understood. At the end of the day, its realization depends on the whole team getting it and putting it into action. So, we must keep it as clear and conversational as possible. Metaphors (in the broadest sense of the term) can be a great way of doing that.

Much of the literature around strategy and leadership draws on military metaphors, naturally enough given its origins. The root word for "strategy" is the Greek word *stratēgia* or *stratēgos*, which refers to "generalship." It goes to the idea of outmaneuvering or overcoming a military adversary, or a political rival or competitor, utilizing available resources and conditions to achieve desired ends. It's essentially a matter of either achieving victory or suffering defeat.

Many purpose-driven organizations do have competitors, or rivals who oppose their agenda for other reasons, and so "winning" can be a valid consideration, but for purpose-driven organizations beating the competition is not typically the main aim. Generally, we're not playing a zero-sum game. Rather, we're on our way somewhere. We're clearing the path to a fuller life for those we serve. If our efforts are a win-win for others in the sector and community, all the better. The kinds of metaphors we draw upon will tend to be more aligned with that intent.

Purpose-driven leaders *lift our sights* toward the future, the end goal. We seek to *rise above* the storm or *get our heads around* the challenge at hand. We *survey the landscape*. We *chart a course*. We consider the *scope* and *boundaries* of what we should and shouldn't do. We look for ways to *overcome barriers* or *cross chasms*. We lay out a *roadmap* and define *milestones* to indicate progress. These kinds of visual-spatial metaphors are more journey-like or navigational in nature and often lend themselves to the quest of bringing about positive change.

And so, having elevated and expanded our thinking, we return our minds to the challenge of navigating the fog of uncertainty before us. We'll do this in three stages.

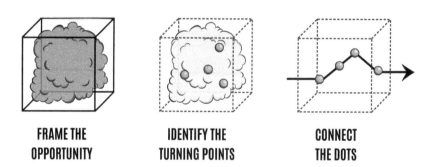

FRAME THE   IDENTIFY THE   CONNECT
OPPORTUNITY   TURNING POINTS   THE DOTS

FIVE

FRAME THE OPPORTUNITY

"How little do they see what really is, who frame their hasty judgment upon that which seems."

—DANIEL WEBSTER

In his seminal 1960 *Harvard Business Review* article "Marketing Myopia" Theodore Levitt used the analogy of myopia (near-sightedness) to highlight the limited strategic perception of many organizations. Those lost in a fog or preoccupied with the fray. He used the example of the decline of railroad companies from their once powerful position in the American economy:

> *"The railroads did not stop growing because the need for passenger and freight transportation declined. That grew. The railroads are in trouble today not because that need was filled by others (cars, trucks, airplanes, and even telephones) but because it was not filled by the railroads themselves. They let others take customers away from them because they assumed themselves to be in the railroad business rather than in the transportation business. The reason they defined their industry incorrectly was that they were railroad oriented instead of transportation oriented; they were product oriented instead of customer oriented.... What the railroads lack is not opportunity but some of the managerial imaginativeness and audacity that made them great."[1]*

In essence, such companies failed to see the tectonic shifts and emerging opportunities that were present all around them because of a

self-limiting frame. They were myopically product oriented rather than focusing on the bigger picture of what the market fundamentally needed. They saw only the conventional set of opportunities from the same old perspective. Had they possessed a deeper conception of their purpose and been able to reframe their view of the space they were in,

FRAME THE OPPPORTUNITY

they might have shared in more of the value created in the years since by companies such as UPS, FedEx, and many others.

This same kind of strategic myopia besets us today, in part for reasons of conventional thinking (and the other challenges identified earlier) and in part because in the modern era with the rapid pace of change, increasingly networked economy, and the blurring of sector lines, we're not sure where to focus and where to draw the boundaries.

We can all use a fresh pair of eyes. There is always benefit in seeing things from other perspectives. Here we explore how we might (re)frame the challenges before us.

Develop Holographic Insight

"We don't know who discovered water,
but we're pretty sure it wasn't a fish."

—John Culkin

Why wouldn't a fish have "discovered water"? Precisely because they're in the thick of it. They take it for granted. That's just the way things are. A fish has no other frame of reference, no alternative perspective with which to compare and contrast the environment they operate in. The same applies in matters of strategic thinking. Sometimes we need to get outside our own fishbowl (or fog) and interpret the situation from other viewpoints. Only then can we see the whole and develop the insight necessary to comprehend what's really going on.

Allow me to illustrate the point with an anecdote. One of the most extraordinary topics I've ever been asked to contribute to was that of stabilization for a conflict-affected country. That is, finding ways of reducing the oxygen available to an armed insurgency—and restoring some transitional level of security and basic services—thereby allowing people to begin rebuilding their lives, and the nation its stability. This is primarily through non-armed means such as aid, governance capacity-building, education, conflict resolution and the like, rather than primarily relying on kinetic intervention. The different sectors (public, private, military, and civil society), with the help of the international community, needed to work together toward that end. To do so they needed some common understanding, language, and intent. On one occasion there were eight or nine experts in the room from a mix of backgrounds, including the humanitarian sector and the US and UK armies, most with first-hand experience in this conflict zone. In this company I was very much the fish out of water. But, apart from the occasional wave of imposter syndrome, I felt privileged to be invited into the conversation. The convenors were friends and colleagues of mine who specialize in this field. I had some background in international aid and development, but none in a context like this. The request of me was simply to contribute to the conversation as a strategic thinker—to listen, pose new questions, inject some lateral ideas from other spaces, and begin to conceive of new ways forward.

One participant was a recently retired senior army officer who was an expert in counterinsurgency strategy. He was mindful of the need for a holistic solution, incorporating political, social, justice and economic dimensions. He had a genuine desire to understand the insurgency from the adversary's perspective. (Rather than agreeing with their worldview, which he certainly did not, it was acknowledging that they too were human and must have some basis for their actions, given they were also putting their lives on the line). This same desire to understand the enemy also applied to the other stakeholders involved, from the government to the villages where the conflict was playing out and was most harshly felt.

The labyrinthine nature of this country's challenges meant that it had to be looked at from all angles to try to find a way through. The retired army officer described the process as one of developing holographic insight into the drivers of the conflict (and thus into its potential solutions). It's a turn of phrase that resonated with me, giving a new name to something I'd intuitively practiced in other (less dire) matters of strategy but had not previously conceived of in this way.

The word *hologram* comes from the Greek word *holos,* meaning "whole" and *gramma,* meaning "message." A hologram then is a whole message or story, or picture if you will. The word *insight* is drawn from the idea of having inner sight. Merriam-Webster's dictionary defines it as the act or power of "seeing into a situation" or "apprehending the inner nature of things." It suggests a probing mind that looks beyond what may seem obvious at first. The idea of developing holographic insight, therefore, suggests that we simultaneously hold both a bigger picture perspective and have a more intimate, perceptive grasp of a situation's drivers. Think of it as walking around the problem to comprehend it from different angles, both by stepping back to see the whole and peering in to better understand how it works.

In our contexts this principle might involve empathizing with different stakeholders (e.g., customers, suppliers, shareholders, funders, regulators). Or it could be seeking multi-disciplinary input (e.g., economic, social, cultural, political, scientific)—whatever combination of views that is most relevant in the circumstances. New insights are typically uncovered where several perspectives intersect. Each facet is like a frame, a window into the situation. All such frames have some validity if they're looking in on the same issue, each making known some different aspect of it. But some will present a clearer and richer view than others. So, we try different frames to see which will be most thought-provoking and instructive.

Choosing a frame is not just a matter of passively observing and selecting the best of the available views. There is an act of will in this. We are also identifying how we choose to see it—the lens we'll use to interpret what's going on and the posture we'll take in doing something about it. For example, Amnesty International chooses a rights-based frame for its work. World Vision chooses a child-centered frame for community development. The United Nations has a diplomatic frame. Red Cross has a humanitarian frame. Grameen Bank has an economic frame. Government aid agencies have something of a geopolitical frame informing their decisions. All are looking in on similar needs for international aid and development assistance, but all are seeing the problems through a frame that is most relevant and instructive to them, allowing each to play its own unique role. We see this same principle at work in just about every purpose-driven field of endeavor, from politics and civil rights to business and social services. The choice of frame has a profound effect on what we see, what we hold to be important, and how we go about our work.

A problem well framed can be a problem half-solved.

If a particular frame is proving ineffective or is starting to lose its explanatory power, reframing the issue can open new thinking. This is essentially about shifting the focus, the scope or angle, of our perspective to bring new information into the picture or infer new meaning. For example, we might reframe a problem as an opportunity or a weakness as a strength. We might shift from a product perspective to one that's more about customer experience. Or we might redefine the business we're in. Reframing doesn't change the facts, but it may well change the emphasis, scope, assumptions, or emotions around the issue—and therefore change our strategic perception.

A famous example from the political sphere is when president John F. Kennedy said in his inaugural address "Ask not what your country can do for you. Ask what you can do for your country." In doing so he was reframing responsibility, shifting the discussion from one of entitlement or passivity or complaint to one of a mutual responsibility to contribute in bringing about positive change.

A classic example from the business sector was when Jack Welch (CEO of General Electric) mandated that every business unit needed to become the number one or two in their market. He recognized that once a division dominated their market, its growth would slow because of diminishing returns (there being less market left to acquire). Therefore, the subsequent instruction was to redefine the business they were in (with a wider frame) such that they didn't have any more than 10 percent of that larger market. By framing and then reframing their space in this way GE's leaders continually strove to both dominate and expand the sectors they were in, which resulted in substantial and sustained growth.

A project I was involved in related to the economic development of a small, remote Pacific island state. It had few favorable attributes for growth. It had a very small population and therefore limited domestic demand and workforce. It was a long way from world markets. With no sandy beaches and with the waters full of sea snakes (as I discovered first hand), it had limited tourism potential. The unspoken, underlying development question for this island was essentially "How might this remote island nation be made to matter to the rest of the world?" In this scenario the only choice was to come at it from a different angle.

An apiculturist from New Zealand had made an interesting discovery. In the jungle of the island's interior was a colony of disease- and mite-free Italian bees that had been introduced by missionaries more than a hundred years earlier. This was a significant discovery given the worldwide phenomenon of Colony Collapse Disorder, which threatens the existence of the bee populations worldwide and thus global food production because of bees' vital role in pollination. If these two factors (the bees and the island's remoteness) could be brought together in some innovative way, a new development opportunity might arise. The island was reimagined as a Pacific bee sanctuary, a quarantined organic location where bee stocks could be kept pure and ultimately exported to countries whose food chains were under threat. The concept was akin to the Global Seed Vault in the remote Arctic Svalbard archipelago of Norway, a facility where seeds are stored as a means of protecting against species loss. Could something similar be done with bees as well? A potential new development avenue had opened up by (a) looking at the island's remoteness as an advantage, (b) reconceiving these insects as valuable assets, and (c) transposing a model designed for another analogous space into this one. All are examples of reframing.

Choose a Direction

"To the person who does not know
where he wants to go there is no favorable wind."

—Seneca the Younger

Once an organization has a clear purpose and a better understanding of its context, it is time to choose a direction to head in.

Direction itself does not contain the answer to every question about the route we will take, it simply sets our bearings. It may only be a general sense of direction to begin with, but, in a fog, with 360 degrees to choose from, it's a good start. We can refine that course later as we step forward and learn more.

To navigate anywhere we need a minimum of two coordinates: a starting point and an intended destination, a here and a there. For purpose-driven organizations the two key coordinates are (1) why we are

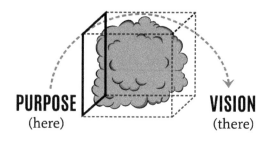

here (our purpose) and (2) what the ultimate realization of that purpose would look like when we get there (our vision).[2]

The arc joining the two is our direction. There's still a big gap in-between. The challenges and opportunities we'll be presented with and the steps we'll need to take remain uncertain. These are the blanks we're yet to fill in. But at least we have an orientation: a territory within which to begin the search for the best path.

We've covered one of these coordinates at length, our *purpose*. But what about the other, our *vision*?

The vision of a purpose-driven organization should simply be the fulfilment of its purpose. A vision is the bookend of purpose. They come as a matching set. If we were to stop and really think about it, why would our vision be anything else? Understanding the simplicity of this makes crafting a vision statement comparatively straightforward. It is our best articulation of what the desired future looks like when we've fully served our purpose. We start our journey with a compelling reason and an end in mind (purpose); we finish it when we have arrived (vision). For example:

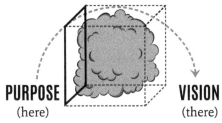

PURPOSE
(here)

VISION
(there)

"To organize the world's information and make it universally accessible and useful."

-Google-

"Access to the world's information in one click."

"To help create lasting solutions to the injustice of poverty."

-Oxfam-

"A just world without poverty."

If you were to invest deeply in this process (as indeed you should), I recommend spending 90 percent of your time on clarifying purpose and 10 percent on crafting the vision—not because the latter is unimportant, but because it is a product of the former. In this way setting the vision (and therefore direction) could be the simplest step in the whole strategy process. Even so, some organizations still make a hash of it. There's a lot of banality out there posing as vision. There are lofty statements that are so cliché or vague or disconnected from the core business that they're more likely to obscure the path than help set our course. Some fail to inspire because people cannot see the possibility of achieving it. In other cases, the vision statement tries to cram in too much (usually a bunch of business objectives), making it long, cluttered, and boring. Perhaps even more directionally challenged are those vision statements that were developed in isolation of organizational purpose, as separate artifacts, there being no obvious connection between the two.

Ironically, it can also be confusing when there are too many "guiding" statements competing for attention. Some organizations produce a raft of such documents—a purpose statement, mission statement, vision statement, strategic intent, list of goals, list of values, belief statement, brand promise, guiding principles, slogans, position statements—believing the volume helpful. Individually each of these statements may have their role and their merits, but collectively they can be confusing if there's an unclear hierarchy. People will turn off if they can't get a simple answer as to how they should orient themselves. It's like getting a convoluted answer when asking someone for directions on the street. When it comes to direction setting, less is more. All we need are two key coordinates: a purpose (why we are *here*) and a vision (a picture of what the fulfilment of that purpose looks like when we get *there*). Together these provide direction, the *why* and the *where*. The rest informs the *how*.

A social enterprise whose history dates to the mid-1800s invited me to serve as the CEO. I was being brought in to grow the organization's strategic positioning, sustainability, and community impact after a difficult period. As it turned out I started just a few weeks prior to the COVID-19 pandemic. The government directed that all the major centers close for what turned out to be months. Hundreds of staff had to be stood down. The management team, who had to stay on to steer the entity through, voluntarily went to half pay and worked long hours. Even operating at such life-support levels, the organization's meager financial reserves would not last very long. At that stage there was quite the fog of uncertainty before us. Like many organizations at that time, we had no idea how long it would last, what the implications would be, or whether there would be any external support. It seemed as though the team tasked with growing the enterprise might end up being the one to shut it down after almost two centuries of service.

Fundamentally, we had two choices: shrink back in self-preservation mode or step forward and keep serving our purpose, even amid such uncertainty and constraint. Although the media continually referred to the situation as being unprecedented, our organization had in fact provided extraordinary service through previous global crises, such as the world wars and the Spanish Influenza pandemic (which collectively resulted in more than 120 million deaths). So, we took lessons and inspiration from that legacy and brought it into today as part of our strategic thinking. We doubled down on our purpose, looking for immediate opportunities to serve the community and our partners in that same fashion. We envisaged what a great outcome would look like in the post-pandemic future and began building toward that. Then, along the arc between the "here" and "there," we focused on the capabilities, culture, and relationships we'd need to develop, providing some mid-term objectives to work toward. Together these formed an incomplete strategic picture during a tumultuous time, but at least we had purpose and direction.

The result? A doubling in size and impact in three years, plus a pipeline of opportunities that could see it double again in the next three. Not only were all staff soon re-employed, but hundreds of new jobs were created. The uncertainty that threatened the organization's very existence was used to strengthen it and take it to the next level.

SIX

IDENTIFY THE TURNING POINTS

"Avoid the superficial, penetrate the complex, go to the heart of the problem, and pinpoint the key factors."

—BRUCE LEE

Whilst the directional arc we hold in our minds might be a clean line between purpose and vision, the pathway on the ground typically is not. It'd be easy if it were a straight road, once we were on it, all we'd have to do is follow it to its conclusion. But of course, it's not that simple. We have many choices (intersections or alternative routes) to consider as we determine the best way forward. Most day-to-day management decisions represent small corrections, an adjustment of the steering wheel if you will, to negotiate a bend in the road or to change lanes. Other decisions, however, have more profound implications—determining whether we'll make it to our

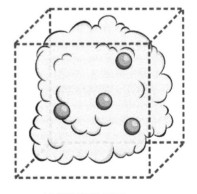

**IDENTIFY THE
TURNING POINTS**

intended destination or head off in another direction. These are the "turning points" in our journey, and in the story we will have to tell.

In this section we look at how to identify these turning points and make a reasoned call. Very simply, it comes down to three things we must do:

1. Focus on the pivotal questions
2. Explore the range of options
3. Make provisional choices

Focus on the Pivotal Questions

"A prudent question is one half of wisdom."

—Francis Bacon

The Value of Questions

In our quest for answers, it can be tempting to jump straight to them. To the familiar, the conventional, or the trending. Or to immediately convene a brainstorming session seeking ideas. But great answers come from great questions, so it's worth holding back for a time and contemplating those more deeply. I equate this slow cooking. Strategic thinking that goes deep on the questions will yield results packed with greater flavor, making more of the ingredients we have to work with. The answers will come to us more naturally, falling off the bone as it were.

The pivotal moments of strategy are more likely to come from a disciplined search for the most incisive questions than from a flash of creative brilliance. The genius is in asking questions in such a way as to open a line of sight into the heart of the matter and therefore, into new possibilities.

*"Sometimes the questions are complicated
and the answers are simple."*

—Dr. Seuss

Questions help us extract the core issues and success drivers from all the practices, opinions, or assumptions that may have previously been applied. Perhaps like a mini out-of-body experience we can be lifted into headspace in which we might think more purely about matters of genuine import, temporarily transcending the noise and pressures below. There's three important ways in which questions help us do this.

1. **Questions initiate the search for new insights**. They demand an answer. Just try asking someone an intriguing question and see if they can resist trying to answer it. Questions ignite our curiosity. The fresher the question, the more likely we are to discover new answers. The more incisive the question, the deeper the answer is likely to be. The more challenging the question, the more creative we need to be. Questions keep us out of the quicksand of complacency and the snare of unchallenged assumptions. They keep us alert, authentic, and agile. They keep us (and our enterprises) growing.

2. **Questions invite others into the conversation**. They attract the interest of those who may have some stake in the answer— our colleagues, frontline staff, customers, partners, and others. They stimulate the exchange of insights and ideas. Questions also level the playing field. That is, by temporarily stepping back from today's answers and opening the topic afresh, one does not necessarily need a PhD to be able to contribute. Indeed, sometimes the most thought-provoking questions are those the executives or experts had overlooked. Sometimes the most

creative ideas come from the fringes. Questions turn strategy into a conversation—one that it is likely to be far more real and insightful than a report produced in an ivory tower. Such conversations are also integral to relationship building and buy-in. It's hard to lead people toward a goal into which they've had no engagement.

3. **Questions simplify and clarify**. If we ask someone a question, we're seeking an actual answer. One that goes to the heart of what it is that we need to know. We soon get the sense that they don't really know the answer (and are probably fudging it) when they give long-winded, complicated, or equivocal answers. The same goes for strategy. Questions help cut to the chase. They test and refine our thinking as we work our way toward the clearest possible understanding of the issue or opportunity. Just as metals are processed by smelting—removing the dross from the ore to get to the gold—so too are strategic insights made purer and stronger through thoughtful questioning.

"Plain question and plain answer make the shortest road out of most perplexities."

—Mark Twain

Which Questions?

The big ones.

Some questions matter more than others. Of course, we want to make good decisions at every level, but first we need to pick out the few questions that will most profoundly shape our overall strategy.

When doing a jigsaw puzzle, there's a couple of things most people intuitively do first. They look at the box to get a sense of the whole picture so they have the end in mind. Then they might typically look for the edge pieces, particularly the corners. By matching these to the picture we begin to frame the task ahead. Everything that follows connects, and happens between, these.

So it is with strategic choices (and the questions that precede them). In this analogy our purpose and vision provide the "picture on the box", an image of the kind of future we're trying to build. Every other decision is in service of that end.

The corner pieces, so to speak, provide the reference points by which we progressively work our way toward the construction of that picture. We might call these our cornerstone questions, the ones whose answers will orient the rest of the strategy. Such questions might look something like these:

- What is our purpose? What do we exist to do? (Purpose)
- What would the intended fulfilment of that look like? (Vision)
- In realizing that, who should we serve? (Target Market)
- How does our purpose intersect with what they most need? (Value Proposition)
- What offerings would best deliver on that proposition? (Products or Services)
- What abilities will we need to deliver those services? (Capabilities)

- How might we best organize ourselves around those capabilities? (Operating Model)

By asking these kinds of cornerstone questions first, we are making our logic clear. The order in which we ask questions is important whenever one answer will affect those that follow (which is often). Thinking itself is essentially a process of asking and answering questions. Therefore, *to order our thinking is to order our questions.*

By keeping these in the form of questions we're recognizing that the environments we operate in are constantly changing. We don't just pose and answer them once over the life of our enterprise. We'll revisit these whenever our strategy needs to be refreshed—such as when there's a significant shift in the external or internal environment.[1] Either to confirm that our current strategic choices are still the right ones, or to revise our approach. In any event the discipline of regularly revisiting these keeps us open and adaptive.

The questions to ask will vary somewhat in each situation. Some will be more market oriented and others more impact oriented. Some will need to ask questions around competitive advantage, role in the value chain, scope of where to play, and the like. The timeframe we have in mind may be shorter (e.g., a five-year strategic intent) or longer term (e.g., a corporate vision). The point is we must do our own original thinking about what is necessary in our situation.

Ultimately it comes down to those questions that simply must be answered (and be answered simply) if we are to deliver on our purpose. Make a list. Condense it to the smallest number of questions possible—the few that are the most fundamental and indispensable, the cornerstone questions. Order them and then articulate them clearly and incisively.

Then begins the journey of resolving those. An answer to a strategic question is a two-step process: (1) identifying the possible alternatives (our options) and (2) selecting those which represents the best fit (our choices). Let's examine each of these in turn.

Explore the Range of Options

"Despite the roar of voices wanting to equate strategy with ambition, leadership, vision, planning, or the economic logic of competition, strategy is none of these. The core of strategy work is always the same: discovering the critical factors in a situation and designing a way of coordinating and focusing actions to deal with those factors."

—Richard Rumelt

The first step in strategic decision-making is clarifying the question, knowing the real issue or problem to be addressed, and why that's important. The next is to ensure we're considering all our options. The more comprehensive our examination of options, the greater our field of choice, and the less likely we are to miss an opportunity or be blindsided. The more innovative those options the greater our prospect of advantage or breakthrough.

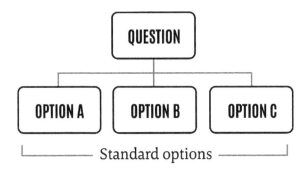

Our minds will naturally turn first to the more familiar or conventional alternatives, those that would generally be accepted as legitimate options in situations like ours. The chances are one of those may indeed prove to be the best available answer to our question. It makes good sense to list them. We might call them our standard options.

A classic example of standard options would be Porter's Generic Strategies, developed by academic Michael Porter in 1980. This posits that there are essentially four positions from which an enterprise can compete: cost or quality and then full market or niche. Competing on a cost basis has to do with efficiencies and keeping the price down. Competing on quality has to do with differentiating yourself on the basis of superior features or craftsmanship. And then within those two streams one can seek to either become the leader across the whole market or carve out and own a focused niche. This is sound economic thinking that continues to have application today, decades after it was first published. If one were seeking to answer the question How might we position ourselves to win in our sector? these would likely be on their list of standard options.

If the imperative is to increase sales, the standard options we might think of first might be to increase advertising, launch a sales promotion, discount the price, incentivize the salesforce, or some combination thereof. Again, these are common go-to options and are worthy of a place on our list. But ideally we want more options to choose from than just the same old levers that everyone else is wrestling over. Otherwise, we find ourselves competing for small incremental wins within a finite space. Most purpose-driven leaders and organizations want more than that. That's why we need to find fresh new alternatives—options that grow the pie, open up new space, realize greater impact, complement not just compete—wherever possible.

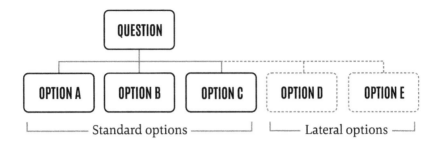

This requires lateral thinking in the manner discussed earlier. In line with the particular question we are addressing, it is about identifying a new who, how, when, where or what.

For example, if the question is *Who* do we want to serve? the search becomes one for a new who. It could be a cohort that is currently being underserved. Or it could be identifying our target customers differently. Instead of breaking it down into traditional demographic segments (e.g., age, gender, location), perhaps we can slice it a different way, such as by what they do (a behavioral segmentation) or by how they think (a psychographic segmentation). Or instead of defining our market by the products we sell (e.g., wheelchairs) we define it by the outcome the customer is seeking (e.g., mobility). Small shifts in framing such as these can open a variety of new options, and more space in which to play.

Growth and impact options can also come from other shifts in emphasis. Finding new whitespace in a market, or the keys to solving a previously intractable need, can happen by making a different question the more pivotal one.

There was a story many years ago of a whitegoods manufacturer from East Asia seeking to enter the consumer refrigerator market in India. It made prima facie sense both from a commercial perspective (given the large population) and a health and social development perspective.

Refrigeration dramatically improves food safety, thereby reducing illness. By extending the life of perishables, the family dollar goes further and allows for a more nutritious and balanced diet. It reduces the time spent on household tasks such as food shopping, freeing up more time to spend with one's family or to participate in the workforce.

The company sent a market entry team to investigate the prospects. A month or so later they reported back to head office. The assessment was that, given the relative poverty of most people, the market was not yet viable, and the company should wait a few more years. The boss reportedly said to them, "there's no such thing as an unviable market, only an unviable product. Now, go and design a new refrigerator that would be affordable in that context." They did just that, making a small, robust, and inexpensive refrigerator—and one that could stay cooler for longer during the frequent power outages. By reframing the most pivotal question from one of demographics (who), to one of product design (what), a new option was created—and subsequently chosen. As the story goes, this led to a faster time-to-market, first-mover advantage, and meaningful benefit for millions of families.

When it comes to identifying options, how we think is often more important than what we know. Nobody carries comprehensive knowledge of all possible alternatives in their heads, nor do they have pre-knowledge of every potential development. Indeed, the great case studies—in business, in social change, and in war—are usually of those who defied convention and circumstances by thinking more imaginatively and courageously than others around them. Hence, the call here is to adopt the kind of divergent ideation we have talked about and then go exploring. There's no need to be tentative about alternatives that might seem to be a stretch or even improbable for, at this stage of the process, we are merely identifying options. Too many is better than too few.

"If everyone is thinking alike, then somebody isn't thinking."

—General George S. Patton

Make Provisional Choices

"Keep your eyes on the stars, and your feet on the ground."

—Theodore Roosevelt

Choices are the turning points we refer to in this chapter. The moments of truth at which we decide to move one way or another at each major intersection.

To this point we have thought *divergently* about our various options. Now it is time to think *convergently*, to assess that range of possibilities, and make a call.

Fundamentally, such choices are based on our perception of where they will lead us. We can only make them with the information we have available at the time. Some are relatively straightforward, supported by clear logic and evidence, and/or the absence of any viable alternatives. Others may need to be made in conditions of uncertainty or incomplete knowledge. Some choices are quite subjective in nature, requiring our best judgement as leaders. In any case, there comes a time when decisions are required of us.

How do we go about this? By focusing on the few genuinely strategic choices that matter most and answering them *provisionally* at first. Let's break this down.

Strategic Choices

A strategic choice is firstly, and very simply, a call made on one of the questions we have identified as being pivotal. It is strategic by virtue of its importance in the overall scheme of what we're trying to achieve. It is a choice in that nothing has yet been determined, and we are free to move in the direction we think best.

It goes without saying that every choice should be considered on its own merits. This includes consideration of the alternatives and the feasibility and viability of the choice, and more qualitative factors such as our values.

A truly strategic choice will consider two further dimensions, which at first may seem to be contradictory, but are essential to one another:

1. **consistency** with our purpose
2. **adaptability** in the future, as that unfolds.

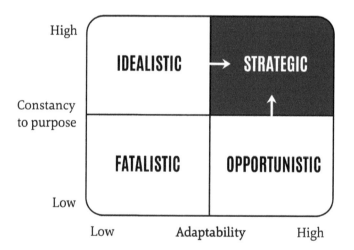

Constancy to purpose is critical to our long-term success for all the reasons conveyed in this book. It is about having that true north in mind in every key decision—and acting accordingly.

Adaptability is similarly future oriented. It is about retaining our ability to respond to an evolving environment and keep moving forward as things (inevitably) change. It is about recognizing that our ideals are of limited value if they aren't put into action in the real world, in a market that is competitive, a landscape that is shifting, or perhaps even into a group of stakeholders who may be hesitant to change. We must meet markets and people where they're at and move ahead from there. Initiative and pragmatism is required if we're to gain early traction. Innovation and agility are required if we're to build on that. Resilience and persistence are essential if we're to keep driving toward growth and impact.

The aim is to draw these two perspectives together for it is that combination of idealism and opportunism that makes the choice more potent. We need both the determination to serve our purpose *through* every circumstance and the dexterity to adjust our approach *in* every circumstance. In doing so we simultaneously make the most of today and build for tomorrow. This is about remaining steadfast in our ideals but being agile in our approach.

Should we fall short in our execution, it's most likely the result of a failure to adapt. But if we're consistent in our pursuit of purpose, at least we'll be failing forward. We pick ourselves up, draw lessons from the experience, and resume the next iteration of the journey.

"I never lose. I either win or I learn."

—Nelson Mandela

An adaptable choice is one that works (or can be made to work) under the different scenarios we may face. So as the environment evolves, we can too.

The adaptable choice triangulates between today's opportunities, tomorrow's possibilities, and our enduring purpose. Whilst we can't anticipate every change that could occur, we can think about the nature of the decisions we're making to ensure they have adaptive potential.

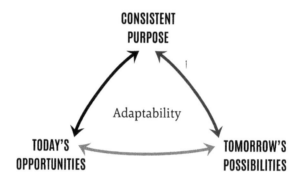

A choice might be considered adaptable if it gives us certainty about what opportunity to pursue today, while at the same time, leaving our future options open. Options are great for they represent a degree of freedom. If we have alternatives, we have room to maneuver. An organization with options up its sleeve is one that is more likely to adapt and grow.

For example, it may be that we have chosen youth as the market we will serve because that is integral to our reason for being. The choice is a robust one in that it will always be pertinent. And yet it can also be adaptive in that it still leaves plenty of room to innovate and adapt in how we serve them as the needs and circumstances change. We've seized the opportunity without painting ourselves into a corner.

If were developing a product or service strategy we might choose to organize those offerings into modules, so that they might be offered in lower-cost instalments, or in different combinations, or be updated more easily in responding to market needs. That too might be considered an adaptable strategic choice that leaves our options open.

If we're thinking about our organization's capabilities, an adaptable approach might be one that considers qualities like the transferability of skills we'll develop in our staff, or scalability of the technology platforms we implement, for example.

If we're considering the kind of culture we need, we might increase the emphasis on regular two-way communication with staff or the decentralization of decision-making or the nurturing of a spirit of innovation to encourage responsiveness. If it's true that "culture eats strategy for breakfast" as Peter Drucker put it, we'll want to be intentional in shaping it in a way that benefits us both now and in a variety of future scenarios.

These kinds of strategic choices enable us to face the future with greater confidence, striking a balance between the near and longer terms. Any change is then more likely to be more of an adjustment than a disruption. Our strategy morphs and flexes more seamlessly over time, being neither chiseled in stone nor in a state of flux. So, the imperative is to really think through the implications and possibilities of each strategic choice and ensure they remain as adaptable as possible.

Provisional Answers

A provisional answer is one that serves the purpose for the time being. It's adopted on terms we believe are reasonable in the circumstances but which may not yet have been fully worked through. Nevertheless, we may proceed on that basis temporarily until we have greater understanding, at which time the choice may either be affirmed, refined, or superseded by another.

We could think of these as working hypotheses, convictions, propositions, or emerging conclusions. Call them what you will, but the point is the same. While we might believe them to be the best answer we have at present, we also accept that they require further assessment in terms of whether they:

- are valid and feasible in their own right (i.e., as discrete choices), and

- mutually reinforce other related choices (i.e., fit with, and add value to, the overall strategy).

Here we remember our definition of strategic thinking which was: "the ability to identify and *think through the set of choices* most pivotal to the realization of our purpose." Because strategic choices come as a set, we must also assess them together, as a whole. In effect we're penciling in our provisional answers, zooming out, and evaluating them as a system. We proceed with care—iterating and refining—until our choices flow well together and have been confirmed as being the best way forward.

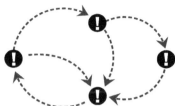
PROVISIONAL ANSWERS

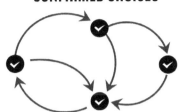
CONFIRMED CHOICES

We make provisional choices to keep us moving forward while still in the process of refining the rest of our strategy. To the extent that there may be some subjectivity or uncertainty in our initial choices, we'd ideally like to test and validate these and back them with some reasonable data where possible.

Depending on the nature of the choice, this could be done through some research or modeling, a workshop, or by socializing it with key stakeholders, for example. Such measures are often reasonable first steps, but they also have their limitations. At some point our decision will also need to find its way into real-world practice before we can be more assured. We will need to learn by doing, testing the market, and iterating until satisfied. In any event, it is best to treat these choices as provisional for as long as we reasonably can before relying too heavily on them.

Some could view this as a tentative or indecisive way of working. But the intent is quite the opposite. Rather than becoming paralyzed by trying to prove everything to the nth degree before making a move, it keeps us alert, active, and attuned. It is learning and adapting reflectively through forward movement, as opposed to stasis.

Provisional choices help maintain intellectual honesty by acknowledging complexities and not over-estimating our ability to know how everything will play out. We should not fool ourselves into thinking that the limits of our field of vision are the limits of what may need to be considered. It's human nature to want certainty. People will seek it out wherever they think they can find it, from surveys to long-range economic forecasts. It's a reasonable thing to seek (credible) foresight to the extent feasible. But it is better to hold to such views lightly than to treat them as proof, for no one knows the future for certain.

Though it may be counterintuitive, one aspect of strategic thinking is learning to live with a degree of ambiguity for as long as that may be necessary. The drive toward greater certainty is still there, but it is sought more progressively over time. Ensuring our choices have some adaptability, and treating them provisionally for a time, allows us to be both idealistic and realistic, intentional and agile, at the same time.

SEVEN

CONNECT THE DOTS

"Great things are done by a series of small things brought together."

—VINCENT VAN GOGH

In strategy, as in much art, value comes from the combination of simplicity and synergy. It works well when the essential elements work together in harmony to produce something new and original, engaging, provocative, instructive, and life-giving.

The beauty of the Sydney Opera House's architecture, Beethoven's Symphony No. 9, or *To Kill a Mockingbird* comes not only from the building materials or notes or characters themselves, but from the elegance with which they have been brought together. The designer, the composer, the author, thought carefully about their subject. They had to decide what is fundamental and what is superfluous, what complements the theme and what reinforces it, when each twist or shift should be introduced, how they unfold, and what they add up to.

Three threads connect these elements: (1) The direct, functional relationship between them;, (2) the shared purpose they're all part of;, and (3) the story they collectively communicate. When these combine, the whole becomes much greater than the sum of its parts—a masterpiece perhaps.

The first thread is relationship. Order and relationship matter. The sequence of notes, the melody, the orchestration, is not just *a* factor in the making of music. It *is* the music, being, "the science or art of ordering tones or sounds in succession, in combination, and in temporal relationships to produce a composition having unity and continuity." [1]

The second thread is the shared purpose which arbitrates how well our choices serve the need we set out to address, and how complementary and aligned they are. Some choices may flow naturally into one another. Or we may discover that some aren't a great fit and need to be sent back to the drawing board (being the reason we made them provisionally to start with). Either way it is a necessary part of the creative process. Each iteration gets us closer to the desired outcome.

The third thread is the story they tell, as seen in the next section.

The Power of Storytelling

"Great stories happen to those who can tell them."
—*Ira Glass*

We have a clear purpose worthy of the pursuit. We have identified and framed the challenge, the obstacles, the opportunity. We have direction. We have nominated the pivotal choices necessary to effect positive change. We have all the elements of a compelling narrative. Now it's about crafting that story.

The development of a storyline is the point at which our choices, and all the thinking that sits behind them, starts converging into a strategy. In effect, a strategy is a story told forwards. Rather than chronicling what has happened in the past, a strategy tells the story of the future path we intend to take. It tells others why that's right and why it matters.

The point of any story is essentially transformation, to move us from one way of seeing and thinking to another. Stories help us see a deeper truth, a bigger world, a greater possibility, a higher calling.

Story is to strategy what a plot is to a play. It sets the scene and establishes those characters who have a stake in it. It connects the dots and provides a narrative arc within which our people and partners might see themselves and their contribution. A story engages and energizes. It shifts the conversation, shapes our outlook, and spurs us to action. It provides the form and flow necessary to turn an otherwise static set of choices into a cohesive, living strategy.

The power of the story is evident in the practices of changemakers. One need only consider the impact of Nelson Mandela's gracious but powerful calls for change after his release from prison or Billy Graham's impassioned sermons to hundreds of millions or Joan of Arc's rallying visions or Martin Luther King Jr.'s oratories or Al Gore's documentary *An Inconvenient Truth* or Malala Yousafzai's story being used to advocate for the education of girls or even Steve Jobs' product launches on stage to see the value of storytelling. Those narratives, and the truths and provocations within them, reverberate still.

The kind of strategic narrative an organization develops is centered around the big questions we have posed: Who are we and what is our purpose? Where are we going and why is that important? And the narrative also focuses on the turning points, the pivotal moves (or plot twists if you will), that will bring that desired future about. However, the story is more than just a list of choices. It's also (a) the connections between them (how they conspire together to achieve something greater) and (b) the kind of message that really speaks to people, appealing to their humanity and imaginations, drawing *them* into the picture.

*"The most powerful person in the world is the storyteller.
The storyteller sets the vision, values and agenda of an entire
generation that is to come."*

—Steve Jobs

Even the most intellectually brilliant strategy is of limited value if it cannot be transmitted in a succinct and compelling manner. Fat research reports or strategy decks crammed with all the facts are fine to have in the background but a simpler narrative is needed at the fore to clarify and convey. If, in the form of a story, a strategy can find its way past the ears or eyes and into the hearts and minds of those who need to be part of it, then it can truly come to life.

Crafting the story is not just something that is done at the end of the strategic thinking process but iteratively throughout. Even during its construction we helicopter upwards to revisit the storyline, and therefore the outlines of our thinking. From there, as we talk through the draft story, we soon sense what's missing—and whether anything is incongruent or too complicated. Whether there are potential threads or connections that would make the overall strategy stronger. Whether it is likely to strike a chord with our intended audience. We keep testing and refining as required, understanding that continually sharpening our plot is essential to the strategy process. Even small, subtle refinements here can have a profound effect on what happens later.

Stories are not only descriptive but also deepening. Customers, staff, funders, and other key stakeholders increasingly engage not only with *what* the organization offers but also *why* they're in that business. They want to know *who* is behind it, seeking assurance that they are authentic, credible, and committed. The who and why are most naturally answered through the relaying of one's story.

Stories clarify and intensify strategies in many ways. They:

- capture attention
- animate our purpose
- make sense of what we know
- present opportunities to make a difference
- tie our choices together as a cohesive whole and place them in context
- build emotional connection
- issue the invitation to join, making it a collective endeavor
- make the strategy process much more conversational, not just a monologue
- give simple form to otherwise complex undertakings
- inspire confidence that our endeavor is worthwhile and achievable
- make the strategy easier to communicate and to spread from one to another
- embed themselves in our memories, meaning we carry those key choices, values, and principles with us as we work to implement the strategy each day

Stories sit naturally with us, and they penetrate. They've been an essential part of culture for time immemorial. It's been central to how we've processed and passed on information, wisdom, and direction—from paintings to proverbs, from Attenborough to Zelenskyy. Every day we listen to stories, watch them, read them, and repeat them. We're more likely to engage with our full attention and whole mind, wanting to know how it ends and what it means. We seem to comprehend the underlying message more clearly, picking up on the deeper truths within. A resonant story stays with us and may shift something within us, potentially influencing our choices and thereby becoming part of our own journey.

The paradox is this: though we shape the story initially, via strategic thinking and considered wordsmithing, once it is released, the story *begins to shape us*. If it captures the imagination, instills hope, and draws others in, it begins taking on a level of inclusiveness, energy, and creativity of its own. At some point the stewardship of the story spreads from just its author(s) to all those who join in its realization.

> *"I have a dream that my four little children will one day live in a nation where they will not be judged by the color of their skin but by the content of their character."*
>
> —Dr. Martin Luther King Jr.

Many stories are about overcoming challenges to realize a desired future. Likewise, a genuinely strategic story is not one that simply assesses the external environment and determines how best to blend in or go with the flow. It is much more aspirational and perhaps contrarian and gritty. It identifies what's wrong with the present picture or what could be so much better. It identifies the key turning points and the calls we are making to change that situation. In this we must decide are we to be the protagonist, the sidekick, or just an extra in this story? Are we merely responding to change or driving it?

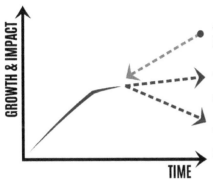

A new story about the future we have purposed to bring about.

The future we fight for in the absence of something new to say.

The future we get if we play a bit role in a script written by others.

Figure 26

In the rest of this section we highlight two different forms of story: the **strategic narrative** and the **grand strategy**. These are only two of several possibilities. Nevertheless, they illustrate the importance of being able to connect the dots and convey our strategy to others in a compelling way. Though somewhat different, the two complement one another. One is firmly focused on the current imperative, the other on the endgame. As discussed, a key to strategic thinking is the ability to combine different perspectives and time horizons for which this is a case in point. It is the intelligence agency and the military commander, the author and the publisher, the

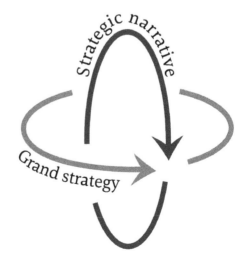

architect and the construction manager bringing their viewpoints together to achieve something greater.

Strategic Narrative

"No one ever made a decision because of a number. They need a story."

—Daniel Kahneman

If you've ever had to make an important pitch, you'll know how much care must go into crafting it. You've only a limited opportunity to make an impression, and the audience is wanting to quickly determine what your proposal is about and whether it is the right answer for them. Every aspect of the presentation matters: the setting, the flow, the insights, the evidence, the proposition, the ask. Every word, every number, paints a picture. So, we painstakingly fine-tune that presentation until we've nailed it.

A pitch encapsulates the strategy, for it addresses the pivotal questions we asked ourselves in its development, and which are likely the same ones that'll be on the minds of our stakeholders. It succinctly articulates the purpose and the vision, the problem and the solution. The pitch carries our conviction that transformative change is indeed possible. This is wrapped in a persuasive narrative that appeals to both our rational and intuitive minds.

In preparing the pitch we may uncover inconsistencies in our thinking or elements that do not reinforce one another as well as they might. We anticipate the questions we're likely to be asked and may realize that we've missed a critical point. Conversely, we may identify detail that isn't adding any value and is just taking up precious space, so we pare it back to the essential insights and choices that make all the difference to both the issue and to the audience. In doing so, we recognize that the development of our story is not just an exercise in communication at the end of our strategic thinking process but also an essential discipline in shaping, testing, and iteratively refining it throughout. It is core to the whole strategic thinking process and is not just an add-on.

> *"If you can't explain it simply,*
> *you don't understand it well enough."*
>
> —Albert Einstein

When crafting a strategic narrative or story, we need to make it as clean and concise as possible. It must outline the purpose we're pursuing—including its context and the crisis, injustice, or opportunity that compels us forward. It must answer the key questions: Why us? Why now? The journey may mean leaving the safety of a known shore to go after something greater. There will be forces to resist or harness, obstacles to navigate, dilemmas to resolve, and proverbial dragons to slay. There are capabilities to develop, choices to make, and critical events that need to happen before bringing it all to a satisfying resolution. These elements naturally lend themselves to a storytelling format, tied together in a narrative arc similar to a movie script. For example, the outline might look like this:

CONTEXT ⟶ CONFLICT ⟶ CHALLENGES ⟶ CLIMAX ⟶ CONCLUSION

The parallels between the creative and strategic expressions of this are clear:

	Narrative arc…	
	… for a movie pitch	**… for a strategy pitch**
Context	Exposition introducing the audience to the story. The scene is set and the main characters are established.	Essential context is established, including who we are, the space we're in, our driving purpose, and the timeframe we're looking at.
Conflict	The inciting incident, the event that triggers the quest that subsequently ensues.	The crisis, gap, or need we must address. The case for action.
Challenges	The tension rises as unexpected challenges or obstacles are presented. The audience sees that the situation is more complex or grave than it first appeared.	The forces against us. The opposition we must face. The barriers we must overcome. The search for options.
Climax	The point of greatest tension at which the key twists and sub-plots converge. A truth is faced and a pivotal choice is made that could make or break those involved.	The insight, foresight, framing or opportunity that opens the possibility of a breakthrough. The vision for a better future. The direction we're going.
Conclusion	The resolution (or denouement) is in sight as a result of the protagonist's actions. Things start to fall into place, closing the loop on where it all started. We begin to see how the quest has changed the characters and their world.	The answer. The set of strategic choices that provide the way forward. We build confidence that the purpose will indeed be served, and realization of the vision is a genuine possibility.

A strategic narrative with a credible basis for hope is always important but doubly so in a purpose-driven organization. There's typically a higher degree of difficulty involved, given the complexities of the social, health, environmental, or other issues we may be seeking to address. And we must simultaneously keep one eye on financial sustainability, especially when operating in sectors where resources are harder to come by. This makes the job at least twice as hard as that of the proverbial widget manufacturer, for whom the quantifiable metric of profit might be the principal focus. For the purpose-driven organization the definition and drivers of success are usually much more nuanced than that and so qualitative factors (and therefore a narrative) tend to play a stronger role.

This is not to say that the numbers aren't important. Substantiation is essential. In the absence of supporting evidence, the story is much harder to accept. The more credible the foundation, the stronger the proposition we build on it. The numbers are even more important when engaging those whose contribution is framed in those terms (investors or funders or CFOs, for example). They'll definitely want a fact base and some plausible projections. Even so, there's something else they need first. Like every human, they need to know what this is about and why it's a priority. They need to know who you are and why you're best placed to achieve the desired outcomes. That is, they need a storyline that connects the dots and places everything in context.

So, we need both narrative (a sense-making story) and numbers (supporting facts). Neither are sufficient in themselves, being interdependent. However, one frames the other and so plays the higher-order role. The narrative leads, and the numbers support that story. The narrative defines what counts; the numbers count that which matters.

There can be pressure to reverse this order. Some people want everything to be evidence based, quantified, and modeled. The underlying assumption seems to be that if it can be expressed as a number it is more reliable. But this sometimes misses the mark. To discount the value of intangible factors such as vision, innovation, courage, relationships, trust, and entrepreneurialism is to lose sight of how progress happens in the real world—and to pretend that everything can be proven ahead of time. It is to assume that all forms of value or incentive are ultimately economic in nature. That strategy is a purely deductive, intellectual exercise and not also a creative one.

Moreover, there are times when strategy can also be a moral endeavor. The purpose-driven organization may choose to pursue a certain outcome *in spite of* the forces against them. They might go for it simply because there's an injustice that needs to be set right and someone must try to even up the odds. Sometimes there are people who need our help who have no ability to pay us and so no economic case can be made. For all these reasons we need a balanced approach with narrative and numbers each playing their appropriate role. Strategies absolutely should be grounded in facts and figures, *to the extent possible*, but no more than that lest we develop a false sense of security in something that might be more tenuous in reality than it appears on paper.

> *"Be passionate about solving the problem,*
> *not proving your solution."*
>
> —Nathan Furr

Beyond the few certainties in life, there are only possibilities. Strategic thinking weaves a story from them both. We lay out a way forward with the best insight, imagination, information, and judgement available at the time. In most cases we cannot guarantee that everything will work before embarking on the journey. Even carefully designed and tested technical solutions still experience bugs after they go live. Hence, our task is to make those choices work and fix any issues as they arise. A narrative holds these elements together as an integrous whole—the proven and the yet-to-be-proven—allowing us to move forward whilst still learning and refining as we go. In that sense the strategic narrative is an ongoing work, crafted iteratively through both aforethought and reflection, and through adaptation in the messiness of the in-between.

In strategy, as in an engrossing story, there is tension. Between what is known and what is unknown. Between what currently is and what could be. Between taking care of today's business while building for tomorrow. Between a trend that's nudging us in one direction, and a purpose calling us in another. In essence the tension is between the desirability of our goal and the viability of our options.

There is a point in the middle at which our minds may be stretched by the array of possibilities before us and the plethora of issues and constraints we've uncovered. As with a story arc, this is the point of rising tension, where we realize the situation is more challenging and complex than first thought. It's like the moment in the movie *Jaws* when, upon seeing the sheer size of the approaching shark, Chief Brody says with dramatic understatement, "you're gonna need a bigger boat."

The resolution of this tension comes from bringing together an understanding of the way things *should be* (the right and best outcome to aim for) and what *can be* made possible in the circumstances. The intersection will hopefully contain one or more breakthrough insights or innovative twists that enable us to go further and be more effective than might have been the case had we not wrestled our way through the complexities. At the very least we look for the most principled form of pragmatism available in the circumstances. Either way, working through these tensions helps us sharpen our story, and hence our strategy.

"The reasonable man adapts himself to the world; the unreasonable one persists in trying to adapt the world to himself. Therefore, all progress depends on the unreasonable man."

—George Bernard Shaw

Grand Strategy

"History will be kind to me, for I intend to write it."

—Winston Churchill

Grand strategy is a big-picture map we carry in our minds to help make sense of where we are in relation to our end goal. It provides a high-level view of the moves we hope to make going forward, as in a game of chess.

The concept is most associated with major conflicts, such as World War II. It is the elevated view of how the leadership ultimately expects to achieve victory over the full course of the war, as opposed to a particular battle or campaign. It encompasses the key elements and choices that must be brought together into a cohesive whole. A grand strategy answers big questions like What is at stake? What does victory look like? What must we prepare for? Who must we partner with? How will our industry and citizens be mobilized? What new capabilities should we develop? How will roles need to change? What happens after we've won? How will a new order—one that maintains the peace—be brought about?

We might think of grand strategy as being more Churchill than Montgomery, more Roosevelt than Patton.

This is not a remote or clinical exercise. It is not simply poring over a map, moving some flags around and then retiring for brandy and cigars in the evening. Neither is it assuming the kind of perfect wisdom or foresight that would see the victor avoid mistakes along the way.

This kind of strategy includes reasoning and analysis but requires more. It combines both vision *and* realism, intelligence *and* intuition, principles *and* pragmatism, adaptability *and* determination. It is both a strategic birds-eye view of the whole and *das fingerspitzengefühl* (situational awareness or having one's finger on the pulse). It transcends the immediate turbulence or setbacks and looks to what will ultimately bring about the desired future. Yet far from being aloof, it is also more human in that it is concerned with what is meaningful, what is right, what ought to be valued and preserved, what brings people together, and what will best serve the welfare of those involved.

Lessons from Churchill

Winston Churchill was more than just your average politician. He was an accomplished historian and writer, even winning the Nobel Prize for literature. He served as a soldier and war correspondent in theatres as diverse as Cuba, India, Sudan, and South Africa. In politics he was a social reformer in amongst various economic and defense roles. He was a direct descendent of the Duke of Marlborough, the leader of the wars that halted Louis XIV's attempts to dominate Europe in the early eighteenth century. All of this—including lessons drawn from various difficulties and mistakes—gave him a well-developed sense of the bigger picture. A more holistic understanding of geopolitics, war, alliances, economics, history, and the interplay between them. Observing the developments in the 1930s in the lead up to what would become World War II, Churchill could place events within a longer historical arc than contemporaries who were only concerned with the immediate politics of the day. He could detect larger patterns and make connections others did not see. He could wrap this into a narrative that made the future threat clearer to others, creating a warranted sense of urgency. As a result, he played a pivotal role in shaping history.

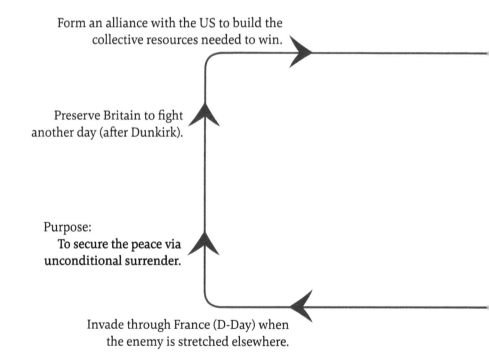

Form an alliance with the US to build the collective resources needed to win.

Preserve Britain to fight another day (after Dunkirk).

Purpose:
To secure the peace via unconditional surrender.

Invade through France (D-Day) when the enemy is stretched elsewhere.

Interestingly, during a ten-year wilderness period out of cabinet between the world wars, Churchill wrote a multi-volume biography of the Duke of Marlborough, which was essentially a story of grand strategy: how Britain, together with its allies, won the overall war against a tyrant trying to take over much of Europe in the early 1700s. As it turns out, this was remarkably prescient, with Winston Churchill having to lead his nation in analogous circumstances more than two hundred years later. Churchill's overall strategy for winning World War II might be summarized in the figure below.

Although this is framed at a geostrategic level, every diplomat, senior officer, soldier, pilot, sailor, munitions factory worker, air raid warden, fireman, or nurse would have been able to locate their contribution

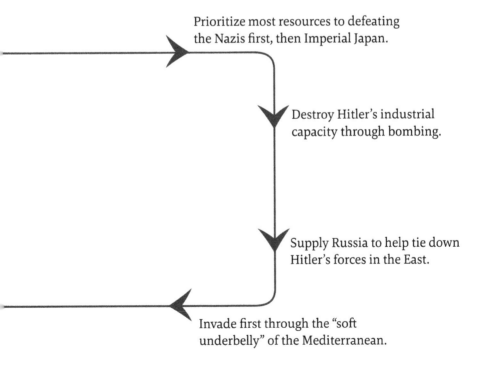

Prioritize most resources to defeating the Nazis first, then Imperial Japan.

Destroy Hitler's industrial capacity through bombing.

Supply Russia to help tie down Hitler's forces in the East.

Invade first through the "soft underbelly" of the Mediterranean.

within that bigger picture. Everyone was invested in the outcome. Hence it provided the basis for remarkable cohesion, resilience, and perseverance.

Of course, the reality was not as neat and linear as represented here. Some plans were frustratingly delayed. Some had their seeds sown years in advance. Some moves may have been regarded as mistakes in hindsight. All came at massive cost. But, for all its ups and downs, his overarching grand strategy remained a robust guide to victory.

As the wartime prime minister, Churchill would have made many decisions on all manner of military, economic, political, and social policy matters every day. There would have been overwhelming volumes of information to contend with and long lines of people wanting to see him or get something from him. There would have been bad news from the front and criticism from within. And yet somehow above all this he needed to maintain strategic clarity on what end every decision was ultimately serving. So his grand strategy provided an outline and some bearings with which to navigate the fog of war while still retaining the flexibility to address the immediate needs of the situation at hand.

Within such a framework Churchill also clearly understood his role as a leader. He knew he had to define the nature of the road ahead, to put events in a wider context and build a narrative around that— allowing everyone to find their place within the story. He had to inspire the people and sustain morale, to form and maintain key relationships, to hold shape and hold firm. Though these might be considered "soft" elements, they were crucial to winning the war and are what Churchill is best remembered for.

By all accounts Churchill was a brilliant man, and as we know, he was deeply determined and inspiring. But like any of us, he had his flaws. He didn't always win, and he made his share of misjudgments, sometimes with devastating consequences. He had to eat humble pie and adjust his thinking many times as the war unfolded. He suffered heart attacks and, no doubt, much heartache. But for all that, he served and achieved his nation's purpose. In the end he, his people, and the allies won. He played a critical role in holding the collective effort together—in large part because he possessed an overarching narrative and sense of resolve, the binding agent of which was an unwavering sense of purpose.

> *"I have nothing to offer but blood, toil, tears, and sweat.*
> *We have before us an ordeal of the most grievous kind. We have*
> *before us many, many months of struggle and suffering.*
> *You ask, what is our policy? I say it is to wage war by land, sea,*
> *and air. War with all our might and with all the strength God*
> *has given us, and to wage war against a monstrous tyranny never*
> *surpassed in the dark and lamentable catalogue of human crime.*
> *That is our policy. You ask, what is our aim? I can answer in one*
> *word. It is victory. Victory at all costs—Victory in spite of all*
> *terrors—Victory, however long and hard the road may be,*
> *for without victory there is no survival."*

—Winston Churchill

Applying Grand Strategy to Our Purpose

This type of strategic thinking, driven by a compelling sense of purpose, set within a bigger frame, and narrated by a leader, is relevant for us albeit on a smaller scale. It is grand in the sense of being a *macro* or *meta* perspective that links and guides the various subsidiary strategies and plans that follow. It surveys the subject from a higher perspective, above the fog as it were, rather than from within it. It is necessarily a more abstract view, but the benefit is that we get a better sense of the whole and the goal. We can see the fuller range of options, consider how alternative scenarios might play out, and think several steps ahead. This in turn helps us connect the dots in a way more likely to get us through to the other side.

Grand strategy thinking has a wider scope and longer term in mind. In the geostrategic context it's not only about how a state wins the war but also how it secures a lasting peace and future prosperity beyond that. A grand strategy employs a more comprehensive portfolio of levers than just military means. It brings in the full array of diplomatic, economic, industry, social, aid, alliance, and other options to achieve its goals. Essentially anything and everything (including the unconventional) needed to develop a satisfactory solution.

In our cases, we might look beyond the boundaries of our own organization to see the whole system of actors whose purposes are complementary to ours, opening the possibility of collaboration. That is, take more of a systems leadership approach. Or we might foresee our sector becoming saturated or less relevant in the future and decide to reframe the business we're in. Or we might begin positioning our organization in adjacent spaces with higher growth and/or impact possibilities.

Another option is to look differently at the capabilities we have or need internally. For example, if we believe that we'll need to develop public-private partnerships in the long term, we might start developing competencies now in government relations, advocacy, and program management. If the decade ahead will demand greater creativity and agility, we might begin a staff innovation program now or begin setting aside more provision for research and development. If we can see that our pursuit of purpose will be intergenerational, we might do more to develop the next cohort of leaders—ensuring they become culture-bearers equally as committed to the cause as we are. Such changes tend to have long lead times so early preparation is especially important.

This higher level, longer term, and more comprehensive, perspective may not be a particularly detailed one, but it does help us place today's efforts in their wider context. It gets us moving in the right general direction. It helps ensure today's choices are building toward tomorrow and are collectively adding up to something greater.

Finding headspace for this type of approach isn't always easy. But it's not nearly as time-consuming as finding oneself being continually tossed around by circumstances, nor as challenging as being unprepared for a foreseeable disruption, nor as frustrating as being outplayed by a lesser rival, or settling for having a marginal impact when it could have been far more profound.

There is no universal theory of grand strategy, no one-size-fits-all playbook, no paint-by-numbers methodology. The approach needs to be bespoke, designed specifically for the purpose and context at hand. There is no substitute for really thinking it through. The answers can only be found through insight and foresight and wisdom and creativity, all of which will defy any attempt to reduce them to a formula. We must do the hard work of exploring the what ifs, what abouts, and if thens.

That said, it's hard to begin with a blank sheet. Below is just one way of looking at it, and a highly simplified one at that. Push it aside if it's not useful in your situation. Or adapt it to your heart's content if it does help get the strategic conversation and thought processes flowing. Either way it serves as a thought-starter, continuing from the Churchill example, incorporating some of the basic qualities of grand strategy.

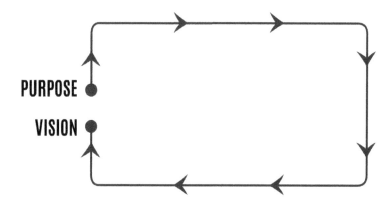

As in the WW II analogy, this figure also is represented as a return arrow. In the big picture the **vision** *is* the realization of the **purpose** we set out to achieve. They are synonymous—essentially a closing of the loop.

Representing it this way is also a reminder of two other important considerations. First, each of our choices and actions need to reinforce others so that the effects are cumulative, creating a virtuous cycle. Second, strategy is an iterative and always-on thought process. We never stop learning and refining.

As important as vision is, in practice it's often framed in high-level terms. The desired state may be some way off, and because we can't precisely predict what that future looks like, we necessarily leave something to the imagination. That is fine for general inspirational or directional purposes but may not be sufficiently clarifying for a strategy. Hence, we often need to define a more specific, mid-term **strategic intent**, an interim outcome to achieve, a "hill to take" that is consistent with our purpose, worthwhile in its own right, and which puts us in prime position to go on to realize the fuller, longer term vision.

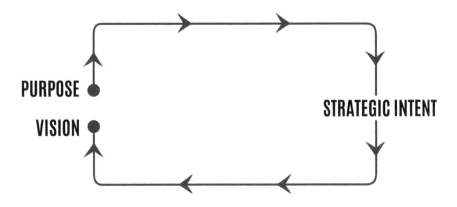

The top arc (between the purpose and strategic intent) represents how we propose to **create value and impact**. These are the pivotal choices, the turning points we have worked through, the dots we have connected. This goes to the big questions like: Where will we focus? Who do we want to serve? How will we reach them? What will we offer? The answers to such questions are to satisfy ourselves and others that we can indeed get into a position to overcome the problem or seize the opportunity that gave rise to our quest. (And that meaningful progress— and worthwhile economic and/or social returns—can be generated within an acceptable timeframe.)

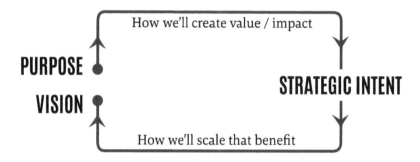

The lower arc (between the interim strategic intent and the fuller vision) might be more focused on how we subsequently **sustain growth** and **scale the impact**. This might be through any number of means ranging from expanding into new markets to influencing policy change to digitizing the services so they reach more people at lower cost. Having created benefit for some, we'll inevitably want to make it available to more—and begin to reshape the sector, society, or environment for the better. Only then can we truly say that we're on our way to fulfilling our purpose and realizing the vision.

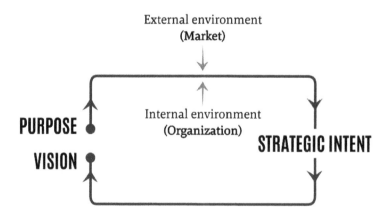

In this conceptualization, the loop represents the strategic path we are choosing to take in its broadest terms. This line also demarcates the boundary between our **internal organization** and our **external market**. Inside the line is the organization itself, its people and capabilities. Outside is the market space in which we're operating. At each point along the line—with each choice we make—we're interacting with the world around us. At this interface we consider things such as what functions we perform (internally) and what we outsource or partner on (externally). What our employee value proposition is (internal) to the talent market (external). What kind of culture and capabilities (internal) are needed to best serve customer needs (external). Whether the way we are organized internally is sufficiently agile to keep up with what's changing externally. Whether we fund growth from internal resources (e.g., retained capital) or external sources (e.g., debt financing). The list goes on. Such considerations are core to formulating strategy.

If we were to bring all those elements together, conceptually it might look something like this:

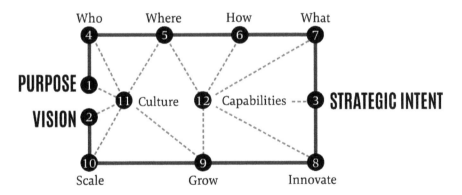

In this example, the flow of questions we ask ourselves might be:

1. What is our enduring purpose? (Purpose)
2. What does the successful realization of that ultimately look like? (Vision)

3. In the interim, what position do we need to occupy so that vision becomes more achievable, and progress more tangible? (Strategic Intent)

4. Who will we choose to serve in bringing this about? Who are we to them? What need are we seeking to address?? (Who)

5. Where will we need to play to do this? Which part of the value chain? (Where)

6. How will we do that in a sustainably advantageous way? (How)

7. What specific offerings will we take to market? (What)

8. How will we keep innovating and improving in order to stay in front? (Innovate)

9. How will we sustain growth over time? (Grow)

10. How might we scale our model, beyond just incremental organic growth, so as to realize the fuller vision? (Scale)

11. What kind of culture and values do we need to successfully play in this space? (Culture)

12. What organizational capabilities will we need to have if we're to deliver on this? (Capabilities).

The questions you may need to ask in your own context may differ somewhat from these. The order in which you ask them might be rearranged. You may be able to provisionally answer some but need to go exploring further to answer others. It may be a little messy as you reorder and iterate your thinking. That is 100 percent OK and par for the course. Strategic thinking is not a formulaic or linear exercise. What does matter, however, is that you identify and answer the questions most pertinent to the achievement of your purpose, give order to your thinking, and be able to convey that story to others. The idea of grand strategy can be incredibly helpful in doing so.

PART III

LEADERSHIP AGILITY

"You manage things; you lead people."
—REAR ADMIRAL GRACE HOPPER

We have a purpose that drives us, and, hopefully now, we have greater strategic clarity about how best to pursue that. There is just the small matter of translating that into action! That can be daunting, particularly if we have significant challenges or inertia to overcome, or if the road ahead is a long one. But it's less so once we're clear on the true nature and role of *leadership* itself (vis-à-vis *management*).

Bottom line, leadership is about commissioning and empowering *people* to serve a worthy *purpose* in a collaborative way. Our role as leaders is to create an environment in which they: align with that raison d'être and its desired ends, grasp the strategic choices made as to how to get there, invest their talents and best efforts in delivering on those, work together in right relationship with one another, and grow as they go.[1]

At first it might seem contradictory to say that we need both constancy to purpose on the one hand and agility on the other. But in practice they're interdependent because we pursue those steadfast ends in dynamic environments. Agility seizes upon emerging opportunities to bring our purpose to life, often in circumstances that we could not have anticipated. A consistent purpose ensures those moves add up to something greater—providing cumulative value, meaning, cohesion, and longevity.

In the movies great leaders might stereotypically be portrayed as larger-than-life personalities—tall and attractive, self-confident and assertive, eloquent and charming. They are people who command a room as they walk into it, mesmerizing us with every word as they take the microphone up on stage. Indeed, in real life, a few do seem to have a natural gift in this regard. Such traits are nice to have if you've got them! But they count for little when the going gets tough, when one's ego needs to take a back seat, or in any other circumstance when real direction, support, and guidance are needed. Effective leadership is about substance not superficialities.

Leadership is not just (or not necessarily) about positional authority. It can also come in the form of thought leadership or the moral standing needed to draw people together. Or it can be at the ground level in the form of mentorship, coaching, counseling, and role modeling (leading by coming alongside). It is about encouraging others toward purpose.

This puts authentic leadership within reach of us all. One's outward characteristics matter less than what's on the inside, from whence our true nature and motivation springs. It's more about the active ingredients within the pack than the label or advertisement. Clarity and determination, integrity and values, empathy and care, all flow from the inside out. Such qualities point *to something greater than oneself* rather than *to* oneself. Hence, leadership is more an outlook, a virtuous motive, an orientation of the heart. All people of character and goodwill, who themselves serve a worthy purpose, have the potential to lead.

There's a wide array of literature out there unpacking the aspects of leadership, some of it immensely valuable. There's no need to repeat those insights here. Instead, here we focus on a few of the qualities for which there is a heightened need when it comes to leading purpose-driven organizations in particular. In keeping with the proposition of this book they represent core principles, more so than the *théorie du jour*. But that is what makes them powerful. They are enduring truths intimately connected to the nature of purpose but from which it is all too easy to drift, given the ever-present temptation of ego or expediency.

EIGHT

CONNECT PEOPLE TO PURPOSE

"In leadership writ large, mutually agreed upon purposes help people achieve consensus, assume responsibility, work for the common good and build community."

—JOSEPH ROST

I f an organization is essentially a group of *people* coming together for a shared *purpose*, the primary role of its leaders must be to foster the connection between the two. Both our hearts and minds (so that there is shared understanding and intent) and our efforts (so all are aligned in working toward the same end). How do we do that? By

- championing a purpose worthy of our shared commitment *(Consistency of Purpose)*,
- making clear choices that drive progress toward that end *(Strategic Clarity), and*
- helping people unite, learn, and adapt as the journey unfolds *(Leadership Agility).*

In this regard the topic of leadership did not start in this final chapter of the book, but from the very first page. We're already most of the way there!

Leadership is not an end in itself, a ladder to climb, or a set of techniques. Because it is about people not things, leadership is inherently relational in nature. And because people are generally smart, with well-developed radars for pretense and double standards, it must be genuine. Hence, the most valued traits we typically see in studies, and in life, will be those that facilitate authentic connection. Purpose, vision, integrity, humility, empathy, respect, trustworthiness, openness, tenacity, patience, adaptiveness, and the like. All encourage the kind of relationships we need to grow as people and professionals, and as enterprises or movements.

As mentioned in the introduction, customers often exhibit a clear preference for organizations that are authentically purpose driven (all other things being equal). This is even more pronounced when it comes to staff, for their investment in that enterprise comes with much higher stakes—a chunk of their lives. For example, one study indicated that employees who had a strong sense of purpose at work were three times more motivated than others, more than twice as productive, more than twice as likely to be retained, and reported almost twice the level of mental and social well-being.[1]

It's hard to think of any internal priority that would be more worthy or yield a higher return. Once we absorb this profound truth, it will naturally take its place at the center of our role as leader. This is not just something we do when there's a gap in our schedules. It is our core responsibility and should pervade all that we do.

There is a certain ease and prolificacy that comes when something is done in accordance with its true nature, the way it was meant to be. For example, when a carpenter is planing with the grain of the wood and not against it. Similarly, when we're connected to a shared purpose, guided by a cohesive strategy, desired outcomes flow a little more readily. More of the right people join and stay, while those that aren't a fit tend to self-select out. Those core staff collaborate and innovate more extensively. They're motivated to pursue excellence in all they do. In such cases, leadership becomes more like orchestration and less like a tractor pull.

Purpose is like the single pure note into which all the different instruments of the orchestra are tuned. Strategy is the score. Leadership is the conductor making interpretive decisions about how best to prepare for, pace, and play that. They guide others in a way that ensures individual contributions come together to produce something uniquely powerful and moving. But for all the mastery of the conductor and musicians, both essential to the outcome, the beauty they produce starts with a shared commitment to one essential note.

> *"Has it ever occurred to you that one hundred pianos all tuned to the same fork are automatically tuned to each other? They are of one accord by being tuned, not to each other, but to another standard to which each one must individually bow."*
>
> —A. W. Tozer

That said, anytime a group of imperfect people comes together, there's always some potential for friction, for mistakes, or for someone to go off pitch. We're human. Things happen. The question for us is whether we are utilizing every experience—each feedback loop—to strengthen the connection to purpose. Are we retuning into that or allowing the difficulties and distractions to cause us to drift further from it? This is the fundamental difference between leading people in a *virtuous* cycle of growth versus a *vicious* cycle of fatigue. Are we built up through the journey or diminished by it?

Leaders facilitate connection with purpose in four main ways. These appeal to the whole person: our emotional, rational, creative, and social selves.

We've covered story and strategy in the previous chapter (Strategic Clarity):

- The **story** establishes an *emotional* connection between the person and the purpose. The desired response is one in which our staff and stakeholders might say, "I see myself in this story, I'm excited by it, and I want to be a part of it."
- The **strategy** appeals principally to the *rational* mind. It says, "this purpose is not just wishful thinking. It is entirely feasible. I see how that can happen."

Now that we have that gripping sense of both potential and plausibility, there are two more elements that complete this connection between people and purpose. Both are equally crucial in translating this bigger picture into a personal and team reality. Without these our pursuit of purpose will struggle to gain traction, remaining little more than a nice idea.

Opportunity

Opportunity is about opening ways in which people might contribute creatively, in line with their knowledge and talents. Situated within the bigger picture, opportunity zooms into the particular role that one could have personally. It elicits the realization that, "I have the ability and the invitation to make a real difference here."

As a leader, not only do you need to articulate the purpose and strategy at the corporate level, you also need to bring to life what it means for the staff in terms of their role. They need someone to highlight how their function contributes to the whole. They need someone to listen and inform, inspire and assure. Someone to illustrate and model what practical application of the values looks like.

One way is to help staff to think of every interaction they have as a potential "moment of truth" or "moment that matters." That is, to think of those interactions as points in time in which *they* are the difference the customer or the community needs. They hold the keys as to whether our collective purpose is served on the frontline, where it matters most. They have the agency to make a difference, and our trust and support to do so.

By way of illustration, one hospitality chain reportedly has a simple rule that all employees—from the hotel manager to the receptionist, the waiting staff, the cleaners—are asked to embrace. "Do whatever you think is right for the customer in front of you." That is disarmingly simple and yet also powerful in delivering great service. It demonstrates both deep trust in its people and a clear-eyed understanding of what ultimately creates value in that industry. Every moment in every day becomes an opportunity for each staff member to be the one who makes all the difference. It makes the purpose much more personal. How much more profound might that impact be if the person in front of us, in our respective contexts, were someone in dire need? The family going through a tough time, the patient with a challenging prognosis, the struggling student, the refugee feeling stressed and alone and in need of someone to really see them and walk with them.

Likewise, we should enable our staff to be full partners in the pursuit of purpose. Empower them with simple rules or guidelines that they can interpret and apply creatively in their work. Let them in on the challenges we face and pose questions for them to explore themselves. Give them permission to experiment and to go the extra mile. Let them surprise us with their insights, ingenuity, and care. Even if they don't come up with novel new answers, just giving them the opportunity is respectful and motivating and will ultimately yield its own return in terms of staff engagement. And if they do indeed identify new possibilities, or better inform our view, we all come out way in front.

Aside from the everyday conversations we have with our teams there are many other ways of doing this. A staff innovation program is one example. Development programs for emerging leaders is another. You can provide brown bag lunch meetings, town hall sessions, or engagement surveys. Spend a few hours working alongside each team in their settings. Go with them as they meet with customers or clients.

There's benefit in educating staff on the way our enterprise or sector works at a higher level. Help them understand the business model; the economics; the issues, challenges, and constraints. Bring them into the "turning point" choices we've made and help them understand why we decided as we did. Allow them to ask questions and offer feedback on how those choices or their implementation might be refined. This helps move away from the "us and them" distinctions between staff and management and equips more people to become part of the solution.

Leaders who do this close the gap between strategy and execution, in both directions. The strategy becomes more implementable in the sense that it is better informed by frontline experience from people who've been given the opportunity to provide input. The execution becomes more strategic in the sense that there's a broader base of people who really get what we're collectively trying to achieve and why, thereby enabling them to see and seize upon opportunity in their everyday work. Either way the gap between people and purpose is shortened and the link strengthened.

Culture

Culture is essentially the relational dynamic between the people who've come together to serve a purpose. It represents the "tacit social order of an organization," the shared values, beliefs, and norms that guide behavior, unify efforts, and strengthen relationships. A positive culture brings greater energy, cohesion, productivity, and even joy, to the work at hand.[2]

When a compelling purpose, and the kind of communal virtues needed to pursue that, are embedded in an organization's culture, it may reorient thinking from that of the so-called *homo economicus* (the narrowly self-interested person whose driving rationale might be What's in it for me?) to someone whose first question is How can I help?

> *"When people are financially invested, they want a return. When people are emotionally invested, they want to contribute."*
>
> —Simon Sinek

If we're doing it alone, it's all about our own mindset. If there's just two people operating in partnership, it's about that interpersonal relationship. But if there's three or more involved in an enterprise, it starts becoming a matter of culture. The larger the workforce, or more dispersed the endeavor, the more important culture becomes as its invisible guide and glue. It is through those networks of relationships (including, but also beyond, any formal structures) that things get done. Healthy interactions will build people up and bind them together, thereby growing both the people and their ability to have impact.

Employees generally take on those behaviors they see as being relevant for their role and effective in making things happen in the organization. In time it becomes a "how we do things around here" mentality. The cues for that come from what they hear, observe, and experience from those around them—especially from leadership. Hence our role in connecting those people to our shared purpose is to ensure the signals we send are the right ones.

If we look at the basics of how beliefs turn into results, we get a sense of how culture can be shaped:

> **What we believe, we see.** (*Our attention is drawn to what we value and/or expect.*)
>
> **What we see, we say.** (*"Out of the abundance of the heart, [the] mouth speaks"*)[3]
>
> **What we say, we sow** (*into our own lives and those of others. Our words matter.*)
>
> **What we sow, we grow.** (*We ultimately reap that which we have sown*).[4]

There's a chain reaction at play in terms of how our values and aspirations work their way into our words, choices, actions, relationships, culture, and ultimately the outcomes we get. If those beliefs (justified or otherwise) are cynical in nature, we ultimately get a toxic culture in which peoples' lowest expectations of others seem to be continually confirmed, because that's what we're most alert to. Conversely, if those beliefs are directed toward something more noble, and we observe around us an authentic pursuit of that, we're more likely to look for the best and seek to be part of it.

As with any chain reaction the most profound difference is made at the beginning of the sequence, positively shaping the beliefs, expectations, and values held by staff. Relying too much on behavior modification late in the process may be a case of trying to tame the horse after it has bolted.

We can put measures in place like a code of conduct, posters on the wall to remind staff of the organization's values, produce an uplifting corporate video, or celebrate achievements at a staff awards event. These are all fine things to do, but they're unlikely to be sufficient in themselves to change an organization's culture. To have any credibility, and to add any value, the catalysts for change must be emblematic of something deeper, something that staff hear and experience every day, and place real value on. They must represent an authentic commitment to a worthy purpose.

Because social norms diffuse from person to person, any behavior a staff member might observe around them may have some influence, including from their peers. But it's the role-modeling of the leadership that's most influential in setting the tone and the standard, for they are meant to be exemplars who show the way. Leaders don't have to be perfect, only genuine. Everything doesn't necessarily need to go to plan, but there does need to be a consistent pursuit of something greater. The standard the leader walks past is the one they must accept. The way they conduct themselves in small matters, and in the corridors, speaks just as loudly as what they may say from the podium or boardroom. This, more than any program or poster, will shape what staff really believe, see, say, and subsequently, sow themselves.

If we want to foster an organizational culture that serves its purpose, customers, colleagues, and community, we must set the example by becoming a servant leader ourselves.

"People buy into the leader before they buy into the vision."
—John C. Maxwell

The power of influencing norms at this ground level really came to life for me in the most unlikely of places: a favela in Brazil. The leader in question was not a governor, mayor, or CEO, but a youth worker. At that time, seven of the world's ten most violent cities were in Brazil. This was concentrated in the favelas where criminal gangs were prevalent. They drew in many young people for a variety of reasons, but at its core, this was largely about a lack of hope and opportunity. The oath of allegiance meant that anyone leaving the gang would do so at their peril, sometimes under threat of death. Even so, in one city, a group of fifty young people did indeed leave together in search of a better life. Tragically, thirty-five of them were subsequently tracked down and killed. Our colleague, the youth worker, put himself on the line and came alongside the remaining fifteen. He had a simple phrase that he would frequently repeat to them: "There are fifteen of you. You each have just one job. To look after fourteen others." This gave the young people a meaningful purpose and a sense of dignity, agency, and responsibility. It built them up as individuals and bound them together as a team. It established a culture of care that subsequently turned outwards, with the fifteen becoming advocates for others trapped in the same situation they had come from. Over time, more and more joined them. Months later the youth worker's mantra remained the same, but the number changed. He would say, "there are 150 of you. You each have one job. To look after 149 others."

What the youth worker helped them believe about themselves, they began to see.

What they saw, they spoke up for. They encouraged one another.

What they said—their testimony—became hope for others in their situation.

What they had sown, they grew. In fact, it became part of a movement of *thousands*.

The same principles can powerfully apply in our own organizations and communities.

"Don't judge each day by the harvest you reap
but by the seeds that you plant."

—Robert Louis Stevenson

NINE

THINK A STEP AHEAD

"The secret of leadership is simple: Do what you believe in. Paint
a picture of the future. Go there. People will follow."

—SETH GODIN

By definition leadership requires us to be ahead of the game. We don't need to be an oracle or savant, just clear on the questions of Where to? and What next? Indeed, the word *leader* comes from the Old English word *lædan,* which means "to guide" and "to go."

Where to? is a question that speaks to the gap between our current position and where we need to be in the context of a bigger picture. It's a matter of direction. Our job then is "to guide." This is about *strategic leadership.*

What next? is a question about the nearer term and more practical considerations. Having assessed the gap, the necessary direction, and the circumstances, we break it down into achievable increments. Our job then is "to go," to step forward and show the way. This is a matter of *situational leadership.*

The two thought horizons work in combination. One considers the future and the ideal, the other the present and the practical. Both are necessary in working our way toward the realization of our purpose. It's at the intersections that we experience genuine progress.

> *"Luck is what happens when preparation meets opportunity."*
>
> —Seneca

We might think of strategic and situational leadership as being like a stock market graph, with one roller coaster line denoting the daily dynamics, and one straight line indicating the trend over time (cutting through the highs and lows, almost as though it were impervious to all the vagaries or happenstances of each trading day). One would want their stockbroker or fund manager to be mindful of both. To deal *situationally* to extract the best possible value from the day's events, and to act *strategically*, being guided by an understanding of the true underlying value of a stock and its likely growth trajectory.

Similarly, as leaders we keep one eye on the emergent issues and opportunities of the day, and the other on where we are in relation to our intended strategy. In this way we are neither tossed around by the waves

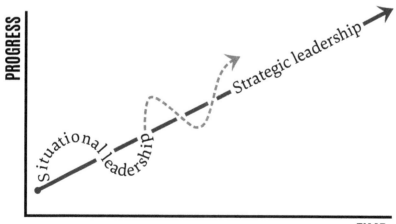

of unanticipated events, nor are we indifferent or inflexible. It's in the reconciliation of the two perspectives that we determine and calibrate our tactical choices and next steps, while ensuring we remain true to our purpose. In this way we can remove a little of the stress (or mania, as the case may be) and keep working calmly and purposefully toward the desired goal. We can be both intentional and adaptive at the same time. That is, demonstrate *leadership agility*.

> *"We are stubborn on the vision. We are flexible on details."*
>
> —Jeff Bezos

Strategic Leadership: Seeing Ahead

> *"The most reliable way to predict the future is to create it."*
>
> —Abraham Lincoln

Strategic leadership is essentially the confluence of all we have discussed to this point. It is a leader who connects people to a worthy purpose, has a sound basis for confidence and can inspire others, and can lay out a clear direction for the longer term.

At times that might seem like some other person, some superhuman, not us. But as we've seen, broken down into its elements, being a strategic leader is within reach for anyone who is rightly motivated and doesn't confuse *foresight* (preparing for the future) with *prediction* (determining ahead of time exactly what will happen). Nor should we confuse *leadership* (moving forward and encouraging others) with *perfection* (getting everything right).

Whether seas are calm or rough, strategic leadership is always needed. People desire a sense of security around the fundamental questions of who we are (identity), why are we here (purpose), where are we going (vision or intent), and how will we get there (strategy). Consistent reinforcement of those points is essential. The more unsettled the environment, the more important strategic leadership becomes. It provides a platform of stability in the midst of uncertainty. In such times it may temporarily stand in for people's own personal sense of clarity or confidence in the future, until they can see and apprehend it for themselves. Thereafter, the conviction of staff and leadership fortify each other.

The extent to which we're able to think ahead determines how well we're able to prepare for both the next stage and the possibilities beyond that. To not do so is either to be frozen in place, or to go around in circles. We may not be able to predict the future, but we can think strategically and soundly about it. Often that is enough if our people have come to trust our judgment, and we bring them into our confidence. And should it subsequently turn out to be a misstep, at least we shared in that choice, we're clear on why it didn't work, and we're able to quickly learn, adapt, and keep moving forward. So, whether we're right, wrong, or somewhere in between, we're still making headway and building solidarity as we go.

In doing this the very first (and most difficult) person we need to lead is ourselves. We must continually remind ourselves of what we've committed to, who we're here to serve, what's most important, the strengths we can bring to the table, the principles and values we've decided upon, the mindset we've chosen, not just at the outset of the journey but at every point along the way, particularly when we face challenges, feel discouraged, or are tempted to go off on a tangent. We're each unique and so what works best for us in this regard will be a little different (hopefully something more substantial than pumping ourselves up with the theme from *Rocky*). But there are at least three things—the major themes of this book—that will be helpful in just about every case. That is to recall:

1. that the secret to success is **constancy to purpose**. Hence, we double down on that and the associated basis for faith that ultimate success is indeed possible,

2. the direction developed through **strategic thinking** is the best available pathway we have at this point, until proven otherwise, so at the very least it's the place to start,

3. that **leadership agility** requires forward motion. Like the rudder on a ship, course corrections only work if we're making headway. Our responsibility is to think ahead, then propel ourselves into that. Remaining anchored in the harbor doesn't get us anywhere. Whether we get it exactly right, roughly right, or fail forward, we are putting ourselves in a position to learn, adapt, and progress. If we embrace that as a natural and necessary part of the journey, we're less likely to stagnate and more likely to actually lead.

This is purposeful *strategic leadership*.

Situational Leadership: Stepping Forward

"I can't change the direction of the wind, but I can adjust my sails to always reach my destination."

—Jimmy Dean

It'd be wonderful if we could take our organization toward a better future along a clearly charted course in stable seas. That might be the idealistic hope with which we set off from the shore, focused only on our mission and intended destination. But, of course, that is rarely the reality. There will inevitably be headwinds to contend with along the way, so we must read and adapt to the conditions as they unfold. Someone must take responsibility for simultaneously maintaining the big-picture view, adjusting course as required, balancing between competing priorities, upholding discipline and morale, and coordinating the practical actions needed to come through in good shape. Not an easy task. Nevertheless, good leaders find the best way to provide both *fortitude* (keeping people connected to the shared purpose and intent), and *flex* (when agility of a more tactical nature is required) in the circumstances at hand.

Such leadership agility is about assessing how the organization is fairing in relation to its environment and intended course—and responding accordingly. A boat's skipper will discern shifts in wind direction, or other potential causes of misalignment, and determine how best to adjust settings in that moment. Often this will involve moves to restore balance (keeping the boat as upright as possible, maintaining an even keel). And they use the prevailing forces (especially the wind in this metaphor) to their advantage. They calibrate a helpful tension between the wind direction and the rudder angle. If it's not blowing in the ideal direction, they adjust the tiller in a way that uses the force of the wind to maintain forward momentum—using it rather than giving into it.

Even though these tactics may require temporary shifts in direction or resource reallocation (e.g., tacking into the wind in a zigzag pattern, or moving more crew to another side of the boat), these adaptations are still purposefully working their way toward the intended destination, even if somewhat indirectly at times.

In like fashion, effective organizational leaders will purposefully step in to rebalance the situation. This is particularly important in the internal environment of the organization. After all, leadership is about people. For example, the more stormy or tumultuous the conditions are, the more our team needs calm leadership. Conversely, if the organization were drifting, the leader would move to inspire a renewed sense of purpose, direction, possibility, and progress. If growth is too rapid, the leader might anticipate a threat that, at some point, the organizational systems and capabilities might not be able to sustain the strain and so proactively move to reinforce those ahead of the need. The sense of urgency created by the external environment can be used to accelerate necessary change internally. In each case the leader is anticipating the likely consequences of imbalance and moving to counteract the threats in order to maintain organizational health, alignment, and forward momentum. Often this requires acting in a manner that is the opposite of what others are doing, staying ahead of the trend, the need, and the currently accepted view. Which is to say, they lead.

Situational *awareness* is knowing what is going on around us. Situational *leadership* is taking charge in those circumstances. Anticipating and initiating the move that restores a sense of direction, balance, and progress—and which may gain an advantage. We can have all the insight and intent we like, but at the end of the day we must *act* on that. The notion that "if it's meant to be, it will just happen" is generally inadequate. More often than not we must step into the situation and play our part if we are to apprehend that promise or potential. In so doing we open the way for others to follow.

That can require a great deal of courage in some instances. Facing down our own fears, addressing that problem we would rather avoid, and putting ourselves on the line. But it will serve to *en*courage others. We do so by either bringing them with us as we step forward or by us coming alongside them to provide counsel, coaching, load-sharing, or some other form of support. Either way insights are acted upon, opportunities are seized, bonds are forged, healthy behaviors are demonstrated, confidence is lifted, and progress is made. When led this way, the team can achieve much more than it otherwise might have. Through the journey we will have grown as people, as professionals, and as protagonists. Why? *Because the people have been brought closer to the purpose.* Not only because we're one step further along the sequence of steps that need to be taken, but also because they've seen it in action, modeled right in front of them. These in-the-trenches experiences can make a deep and lasting impression. They have the potential to fundamentally shift one's outlook and conviction, which in turn inspires others. As an enterprise we will have kept ourselves in the game and kicked off a virtuous cycle of mutual encouragement thereby putting ourselves in position to take the next stride forward, and then the next.

> *"If your actions inspire others to dream more, learn more, do more and become more, you are a leader."*
>
> —John Quincy Adams

While strategic leadership should *think* several steps ahead into the future, situational leadership *acts* in the very near term. It's about the now and the next. We can't be responsive if we're not present. We can't lead people we're not walking with. In this regard it's essential that we don't move too far ahead of those we're responsible for and rely on.

I recall a conversation with the then national president of one of the major political parties that tends to form government alternately with another. He opened up, at a very personal level, about his life and career in politics. He was regarded as a great intellect and someone who very genuinely wanted to get the country prepared for the kind of future it would face. Along the way he'd served in many prominent leadership roles in government and civil society, introducing profound, far-reaching reforms. In many ways he might have been thought of as being ahead of his time. And therein was his major regret. Not everything had gone as well as he had hoped. Some found his policies too complex, too futuristic, too much of a stretch. And in his deep commitment to the nation, he felt he'd traded too much time with his family. "Do you feel that it was all worth it?" I asked him. There was an extraordinarily long pause as he contemplated his answer. We could see the cogs turning in his mind as he reflected on all the triumphs and disappointments over a long and distinguished career. Then he simply and solemnly replied, "No, it wasn't." An astonishing answer, and not something one would ever hear in the media, but we felt privileged that he was prepared to be so humble and honest with us. "What would you do differently if you had your time over again?" I asked. He indicated that he would have continued to think about the long term in the same way but introduced each stage more gradually—thereby making them more understandable, timely, and attainable. Or put another way, one step at a time rather than too many giant leaps forward.

This is a case in point around the need for the right balance of strategic and situational leadership. We need both, but in their right measure and at the right time.

TEN

SERVE THE PURPOSE

"If serving is beneath you, leadership is beyond you."

—UNKNOWN

I t's not enough to have a purpose on paper. We must serve it in practice as well.

To serve is to submit to something we hold to be greater than ourselves. To put our own personal agenda, comfort, or ego aside in favor of other people's interests. Rather than seeking to elevate ourselves, we channel our aspirations through our organization or community as it pursues its collective purpose.

The word *submission* is simply comprised of *sub*, meaning "under", and *mission*, meaning "purpose." It is to come under purpose. To yield to something of higher importance, something that is worthy of our service. We follow, invest in, safeguard, and deliver on the cause we have adopted, one which serves the greater good.

Serving the purpose is about the rising tide that lifts all boats, a form of success in which all those we are responsible for can benefit. The quality and sustainability of the outcomes produced in this manner are far superior to those of the everyone-for-themselves scramble, political one-upmanship, or the zero-sum game in which each player seeks power over others to further their own agenda or ideology. Ironically, the self-serving climb to the top of the ladder ends up being more like a slide to the bottom. If not in the positional titles we accumulate on the way, then in the diminishing of one's relationships and respect, and in the impermanence and hollowness of these short-lived victories.

An authentic leader steps *forward* into responsibility, more so than *up* onto the next rung of personal advancement. In genuinely purpose-driven contexts, the former tends to lead to the latter anyway. The more we serve the shared purpose, the richer we become in terms of job satisfaction, professional credibility, interpersonal connections, political capital, organizational strength, and the ability to get stuff done. We grow in our individual and collective standing not because we have engineered or appropriated it for ourselves, but because others are edified in working with us and want more of what we have to give.

Imagine two different leaders in similar organizations who are equally smart and equally busy. Each periodically visits their various service centers. The first walks around with his hands behind his back, making polite small talk. A brief gathering is organized for all the staff to come together to hear the leader give a corporate update, inform them of a new plan, and drop a few pearls of wisdom. The leader tells the staff they're doing a good job and then departs for his next appointment. It's like a visit from a royal. The second is a servant leader. She has a habit of coming alongside the staff, introducing herself to the few she doesn't already know, wanting to learn more about the person and their work. She asks sincere questions of them, like "what do you most enjoy about helping our clients?" or "how do you think we could make this program more impactful?" and really listens to what they have to say. Sometimes she notices something small that needs to be done, rolls up her sleeves, and goes over and does it herself. She quietly walks over to a client who's looking a little lost or lonely in the waiting room, strikes up a friendly conversation, and connects them to the staff member who can best help. Her brief gathering with the staff is part update and part workshop. She asks for input on some key decisions, valuing the first-hand experiences and insights the staff have.

Which of the two would enjoy greater engagement and credibility with staff? Who are they more likely to want to work with, and to follow? All other things being equal, the one who more authentically *serves* the purpose we say we stand for.

Though it may seem counterintuitive at first, our true authority as a leader comes not from asserting ourselves *over* others but by coming *under* authority ourselves. For example, my son is an officer in the navy. Though still in his twenties at the time of writing, as a lieutenant he has authority over his team of enlisted men and women. He has that because he himself is under authority of the next ranking officer in the chain of command. Further up the ranks, the chief of the military derives his authority from the government. They in turn exist to serve a greater end: the security of the country on behalf of its citizens. Without that higher purpose, there would be no legitimacy to the authority of the uniform. In the same way, we as leaders at any level of our organizations have legitimacy to the extent that we are submitting to a higher purpose—and are demonstrably serving it. Even if one is the founder, owner, president, and chief executive, any lasting influence they have ultimately derives from the consent of those they serve, the worthiness of their purpose, and the values they exhibit. Without that there is no moral authority, no cohesion, and no point. We do well to remember that we are *all* ultimately in service of something and someone greater than ourselves. Purpose-driven leaders should be the most conscious of that, and the most servant-like of all.

"The vocation of every man and woman is to serve other people."

—Leo Tolstoy

If we have an honorable purpose, it should not be seen so much as a heavy burden sitting *on* us as an opportunity in *front* of us, a sense of momentum *behind* us, and an authorizing idea *with* which to engage others. As leaders our first job is to activate it ourselves, and in the process of so doing, encourage and empower our teams to do likewise.

Here we highlight four qualities that are especially important for leaders of purpose-driven organizations. Each represents an act of service in itself, the kind of laying down of oneself that causes others to rise and greater outcomes to be realized.

Resolve is about constancy to purpose through all circumstances. **Integrity** is about maintaining the clarity and purity of purpose, regardless of any temptation to cut corners. **Humility** is about placing the collective purpose above one's personal interests. **Legacy** is about ensuring the purpose continues to build momentum, even after we move on.

Leadership as Resolve

"The truth is a trap: you cannot get it without it getting you; you cannot get the truth by capturing it, only by its capturing you."

—Søren Kierkegaard

To be resolved is to have a matter settled in our minds prior to any challenges that may arise. Having considered the value of what is at stake, we conclude that we must proceed come what may. We are convinced that the quest is worthy of us, so we give it all we've got regardless of whether we subsequently succeed, fail, or simply move the needle in the right direction. To be resolved is to affirm the purpose we will serve and the values we will uphold in its pursuance, thereby abating any equivocation or distraction along the way. It is to be determined to finish what we started and to steel oneself beforehand, as one might for a marathon or mountain climb.

To be resolved can be costly, but it also has tremendous power in effecting change. Oftentimes it's that combination of focus and persistence that realizes the breakthrough.

The level of commitment the leader exhibits also sets the ceiling of what they can expect from others. Lift that standard - role-modelling what the healthy pursuit of a higher purpose looks like - and at least some others will rise to the occasion. We'll soon see who the next generation of leaders could be by observing who steps forward into the aspirational space created between the way things are and the way they could be.

Purpose-driven leaders don't embark on such journeys just for the money, the medals, or because they felt inspired when they got out of bed this morning. They do it because they have been drawn to a truth, a call, a plight, a quest that seems to have their name on it. They do it because it must be done—and because they intuitively sense that it was meant for them. It has somehow captured their imagination, their sense of what is good and right, their desire to grow and to be part of something greater than themselves.

Resolve turns mountains into molehills. If not in the level of effort required to ascend them, then at least in terms of their ability to deter us. And in those times when we do find ourselves walking through dark times, resolve ensures we continue to grow through the experience, developing character and strengthening organizational resilience along the way.

> *"Mountaintops inspire leaders, but valleys mature them."*
> —Winston Churchill

Resolve represents the fastest route to the desired outcome. When we maneuver along the way, with resolve we can do so with greater clarity and confidence, accelerating through the corners as it were. Either way, whether climbing hills, traveling through valleys, or negotiating the bends, we are still progressing toward the goal.

How do we develop such resolve? By reminding ourselves of all we've covered thus far:

- committing to a purpose worthy of our best;
- starting with the end in mind, and keeping it in mind;
- having an authentic basis for faith, for conviction, for confidence that it can be done;
- accepting the cost up front, so we don't waver when things get tough;
- placing developments in a wider context, a long arc of necessary change;

- possessing strategic clarity on those few things that matter most;
- taking responsibility for our part in that—no more, no less;
- bringing our unique gifts to the table, so we're playing to our strengths;
- putting ego aside in favor of the greater good - so we don't become discouraged in those times when it doesn't get fed;
- connecting with fellow travelers and continually encouraging one another; and
- being prepared to be agile so that we're built, not broken, through change.

Bottom line: constancy to purpose is more about inner clarity and commitment than outer circumstances. Remaining resolute can be hard in hard times. To have any staying power our service has to be toward something that is life giving and of lasting value. Something that holds greater power than us and upon which we can rely. A truth that has captured us.

Leadership as Integrity

"Always do right. This will gratify some people and astonish the rest."

— Mark Twain

Leaders lead by holding it together.

The word *integrity* derives from the Latin word for integer, meaning "whole," "intact," or "complete." When used to describe a leader, it refers to someone who consistently holds shape in all conditions just as we hope a ship's hull will maintain its integrity through a storm. They do the right thing regardless of any external pressure to do otherwise. They are the same person to all regardless of their circumstances.

In Mark Twain's observation, doing what's right will "gratify some people" in that it meets the expectations of those who hope for the best. Those people of goodwill who really want to see the organization deliver on its promise. We need ever more of these. Demonstrating integrity keeps others on board, fostering a culture in which they can flourish. Integrity might "astonish" others who've become somewhat cynical through prior experiences. They may have seen so much hypocrisy or politics in some environments that they have come to expect it everywhere. To surprise these people through the demonstration of integrity is to begin rebuilding their trust in leadership and hope for the future. In time they might also join the ranks of the gratified.

If we are to encourage this, we must once again be consistent in ourselves. We must know who we are (identity), our reason for being (purpose), the principles we hold dear (values), and the truth on which we stand (our basis for faith or confidence in the future). It is against these benchmarks that we demonstrate congruity, strength, and dependability in our actions, which is to say, integrity. Without such a framework there is no shape to maintain.

Most people will forgive an honest mistake, of which we, as fallible beings, are likely to make many. But it only takes one major lapse in integrity, one immoral decision, to ruin everything. Reputation and relationship can take years to build and yet only moments to lose. At a bare minimum we must assume that everything will one day be brought into the light and therefore act as people who'll need to give an account. We should recognize those choices that represent a slippery slope and stay well away from the edge. But while that holds some deterrence, it's not enough. That's more about behavior modification than the state of one's heart. Human nature is such that we tend to allow ourselves small shortcuts when we think it doesn't really matter or when we think no one will find out. Such seemingly inconsequential compromises often grow into larger ones. The better determination is to be faithful in all things, including the small. To do the right thing simply because it is the right thing to do. To set our minds on the virtuous and to take every opportunity to put those values into practice including—and especially—with the people others underappreciate and in situations outside of the limelight. For it is here that true character is developed and in which we build more authentic trust and connection with others. This is to see every integrous action as sowing a seed or making an investment in the future. It is to love the good and find joy in it.

New York Times writer David Brooks put it this way:

> It occurred to me that there were two sets of virtues, the résumé virtues and the eulogy virtues. The résumé virtues are the skills you bring to the marketplace. The eulogy virtues are the ones that are talked about at your funeral — whether you were kind, brave, honest or faithful. Were you capable of deep love?

> We all know that the eulogy virtues are more important than the résumé ones. But our culture and our educational systems spend more time teaching the skills and strategies you need for career success than the qualities you need to radiate that sort of inner light. Many of us are clearer on how to build an external career than on how to build inner character.

> But if you live for external achievement, years pass and the deepest parts of you go unexplored and unstructured. You lack a moral vocabulary. It is easy to slip into a self-satisfied moral mediocrity. You grade yourself on a forgiving curve. You figure as long as you are not obviously hurting anybody and people seem to like you, you must be O.K. But you live with an unconscious boredom,

separated from the deepest meaning of life and the highest moral joys. Gradually, a humiliating gap opens between your actual self and your desired self, between you and those incandescent souls you sometimes meet.[1]

We might sometimes see an article that tells us that research shows that leaders with integrity are 43 percent more effective or that purpose-driven leadership is on trend or something of that nature—as though it were a consumer product or fashion item. It may well be presented as a tool or lever for growth. This is missing the mark in my view. The fact that studies may find a link between integrity and positive outcomes is interesting though wholly unsurprising. But if we seek out that quality only for what we might gain from it, we prove that we aren't there yet. Integrity and character have their own merit; they are their own reward. While we might reasonably expect them to serve us better in the long run, that ought not be our primary motivation. If it is, could our leadership values be said to be authentic? Might our proverbial hull be more likely to spring a leak when next placed under pressure? The right motivation is key.

Earlier in life I used to think it an immutable law that if I just try to do right everything will inevitably work out, even if that takes time. I still think that is mostly true but not entirely. It certainly helps in building character and credibility. It helps in not shooting oneself in the foot quite as often. But the fact is, there's no accounting for other people's behaviors or disruptive forces beyond my control. I can only do me. Moreover, *I* may be the one who makes a mistake or inadvertently lets others down, perhaps without even realizing it. The same is true of us all. Recognizing that, we can only take responsibility for our own choices, show grace toward others for their shortcomings, and navigate each situation as best as is possible in the circumstances. Sometimes that's still messy but the presence of turbulence or opposition does not in itself indicate the absence of integrity. Rather, integrity is what's needed in the storm. It is not a guarantee that tempests will be avoided, but rather it provides the inner strength needed to make it through intact.

Confidence in both leaders and organizations is most won or lost in times of difficulty. It is in those moments of truth when we could be tempted to take the more-expedient-but-less-principled path. If we demonstrate an authentic commitment to purpose in all conditions, others will be more likely to lean in and reflect those qualities as well, thereby building our collective culture and reputation. An organization's real values are demonstrated not through their PR-generated headlines, but on the frontlines in the ordinary interactions when the going is at its most challenging, when one's convenience is willingly put aside for the benefit of those being served.

The higher the purpose the greater its ability to pull us up out of mediocrity. The more costly the price of staying true to our word and values, the deeper the respect and relationships we develop. As with physical exercise, moral strength develops by setting our eyes on the prize and repeatedly pushing through resistance, or the temptation to do anything other than the best and right thing.

To have a leadership approach that steps into these moments with a spirit of generosity and grit, understanding the mutual benefit that awaits on the other side, is to be genuinely purpose-driven. To hold shape in all conditions. To have integrity.

> *"A true leader has the confidence to stand alone, the courage to make tough decisions, and the compassion to listen to the needs of others. He does not set out to be a leader but becomes one by the equality of his actions and the integrity of his intent."*
>
> —General Douglas MacArthur

Leadership as Humility

"Pride is the problem; humility is the answer."

—Joyce Meyer

Pride cometh before a fall, at least when we trip over our own puffed-up egos.

Of course, there are positive expressions of pride. Like when we seek excellence in, and take gratification from, our work. When we radiate with respect for our team or joy over our children. But pride ultimately works against us when it manifests as self-importance, presumption, or a sense of superiority. Pride is corrosive when it seeks power and recognition *over* others rather than seeking empowerment and recognition *for* them.

Hubris is the enemy of personal and professional growth. Paradoxically, the more we seek kudos for ourselves, the poorer we become as leaders. If we think we've arrived, we don't go searching for the next advance. We don't open up to new perspectives, discern early signals, or pick up on nuances. We don't recognize that there may be higher levels of value, deeper insights, or better solutions yet to be discovered. Moreover, we put other people off, deterring them from being as open or trusting as they might otherwise be. It leads to fixed mindsets and double standards, pomposity, and politics—all the things we cannot stand about narcissistic bosses or toxic cultures.

The key is in where pride is directed: toward others or us. The latter is fundamentally self-centered, always craving affirmation and deference. Essentially it is paying homage to oneself and expecting others to follow suit. In contrast, humility is a more realistic assessment of where we are. It places us in proper context, having regard to higher purposes and the inherent value and qualities of those around us. It is not to think poorly of ourselves nor to necessarily lack confidence. Rather it is to be seekers of the good and the true and to see ourselves as contributors within a bigger picture. It is to appreciate and value our colleagues and what they bring to the table, recognizing their strengths as well as our own, understanding that we are better together.

Pride would have us believe that others are impressed when *we* achieve and receive accolades. In reality others are inspired when we think more about *them* than ourselves. When we have *their* best interests at heart. When we assign *them* due credit. When we continue to serve the greater good through all difficulties rather than retreating into self-preservation or self-promotion.

We're all imperfect people, working with other imperfect people in dynamic environments. We don't know it all. Some things won't go our way. Our posture, our up-front choice as to how we'll approach this, matters a great deal. If we're stiff with pride, we're going to be defensive and get knocked down. But if we choose to operate from a position of humility, we can be far more agile and resilient. We can either be conceited or real but not both.

Even so, some still associate humility with weakness. Perhaps this comes from the so-called orphan spirit that suggests one must grab recognition and advantage for themselves before others take it. That one must prove their worth and hide their limitations. That the strengths of others may represent competition. That we must protect our patch. The instinct may be to hoard for oneself, to stand alone, to assert primacy, and to resist interdependence on others.

In contrast true humility comes from being secure in who we are. The word *humility* derives from the Latin *humilitas*, which may be translated as "grounded." It is a type of social intelligence. If we know ourselves and others, keep it real, and maintain a balanced perspective, we build stronger relationships. We can act more wisely in both serving and leading others, always remaining focused on our ultimate purpose.

This is far more life giving and sustainable than the alternative. We're free to be ourselves. We're in a less stressful state than having to keep up appearances, pretending to be something we're not. We can lead from our strengths and surround ourselves with coworkers who complement us. We're able to develop holographic insights by combining our perspectives. We create a welcoming, safe, and inclusive culture. We build trust and keep each other accountable. We're better able to mentor others, and we keep learning ourselves. Our opportunities and impact multiply as more want to walk and work with us.

Two opposing experiences illustrate the chasm between these alternatives.

A colleague and I once had the privilege of facilitating a forum of a United Nations body. Various sector leaders and innovators from around the world were to attend. Given the importance of the subject, weeks had been spent clarifying the brief, fine-tuning the design, and confirming arrangements. Even so, we arrived in New York to find that several things had changed, including having additional speakers added unexpectedly to an already tight agenda. At the event one speaker took up more than double their allotted time, repeatedly resisting every signal to wrap up. Perhaps they felt their content was the most important or that this was their time to shine. I don't know, but it certainly made an already tough gig that much harder. We adapted again. As it happened, I was the next scheduled speaker, so to make up time, my session time was halved. Even so, just a couple of minutes in a participant near the front waved insistently to get my attention, looking somewhat agitated. In the circumstances it wasn't appropriate to take questions from the floor just yet, so I kept going. Nevertheless, they persisted to the point where there was no choice but to respond. When I asked what the trouble was, they said, "with all due respect, I didn't come here to listen to you. I came here to talk about me." I was momentarily speechless, not having encountered anything quite so brazen before. It appeared that for a few this forum was seen not so much as an opportunity to collaborate and learn from peers as an opportunity to promote themselves. It was especially jarring given the selfless and inspirational work of so many other outstanding leaders in the room.

What most people will find far more impressive is when an accomplished person is not ostentatious but instead is filled with a generous spirit toward others. One starkly contrasting example that comes to mind was a leader I spent time with in Soweto, Johannesburg. She would have been around 80 years of age and was referred to by all as "Granny." Her women's group had done incredible work over the years. And yet she was inexhaustible, continuing to serve others joyfully through thick and thin. The esteem she was held in was evident in the way people greeted her wherever we went. It struck me as we visited their initiatives (like a hospice for the dying, a nutrition program, and the like), that she never once highlighted her own contribution. She was always assigning credit to others.

Normally I would not be walking around in that particular part of town, being one of the most crime ridden. In fact, some of the gang members on a couple of street corners made it abundantly clear that if it wasn't for the fact that I was there with Granny, I'd be in trouble. There I was, a middle-aged white Aussie male with an elderly African woman effectively acting as my bodyguard! I was safe not because of any positional authority or physical strength she held, but by virtue of the deep respect others had for her dedication to their community. Her service was her superpower.

As her story makes clear, humility is not about thinking less of oneself. It is certainly not about being passive or a doormat. Rather, it's thinking of others more and considering their interests and contributions to be at least as important as our own. It's having security in who we are, love for those we serve, and courage in the cause. (I later discovered that she had received prestigious awards from Nelson Mandela and the Pope for her work—but she never mentioned that to me).

It is from an attitude of humility that we can be magnanimous. By acting generously our connection to the world around us expands, thereby opening yet more opportunities to make a difference. Humility is an essential quality of those who would serve something greater.

Leadership as Legacy

*"David served God's purpose in his own generation,
then he died."*

—Acts 13:36 CEV

This verse sat above my home office desk for many years. It refers to my namesake, King David, who committed his life to something (or in this case, someone) greater. In doing so he overcame adversity, ego, and his own errors, in taking his nation to a whole new level of social and economic prosperity.

Admittedly it's somewhat unusual as a motivational quote, particularly the last three words! But for me it was a reminder of:

- the power of standing for something of great and enduring value;
- the importance of thinking in terms of intergenerational change—enabling others to successfully pick up the cause beyond our time; and

- the sobering reality that life is short, and none of us know what tomorrow may bring.

To be in a leadership role is a privilege, albeit a temporary one. We're there only for a season. The imperative is to use that opportunity for maximum impact while we can. To look for every opportunity to serve the purpose and the people we've been entrusted with.

This raises the question of what our leadership legacy is to be. As executives our performance is typically measured in terms of the quantitative *results* that have been achieved. But the success of a leader is largely about the quality of *relationships* they foster. Indeed, leadership *is* a relationship with those for whom we are responsible. At the end of our time in our position, at the end of our careers, or even at the time of our eulogies, the results we've achieved may be of some passing interest. But what people will most remember is the extent to which we have cared for, encouraged, and developed others—particularly the next generation.

> *"People will forget what you said, people will forget what you did, but people will never forget how you made them feel."*
>
> —Maya Angelou

In our professional lives it's tempting to think of results as being solid measures of success, and therefore primary, with relationships being somewhat soft or secondary. But any agent of change knows they go together, particularly if we want that change to stick. Leaders achieve relatively little by themselves but much through others. We imperil both our purpose and our enterprise if we neglect one for the other. Results are often transitory, their significance fades with time. But relationships—and the impact we've had on others—endures for much longer. Some of those we inspire will subsequently pick up the baton and do likewise. This is our greater legacy as a leader. The ripple effect of our life impacting others.

I had a literal reminder of this principle sitting on my desk as a CEO of a nonprofit organization, part of an iconic global movement that has produced an astonishing array of purpose-driven leaders, social innovations, and community initiatives over more than 170 years. The artefact in question was a wooden baton, like that used in relay races of long ago. Inscribed on it are the names of every CEO since the organization's inception. The tradition is that the outgoing leader will write the name of the new incoming leader on the baton and ceremoniously pass it to them. This signifies that the new leader is being entrusted by all those who went before to carry on the purpose and values of that organization, in selfless service to others. In due course, it becomes that CEO's turn to inscribe the name of the next leader and pass the baton to them. One leader doing this for the next is a significant moment. The cumulative effect of five prior leaders doing that for the sixth is powerful. In my case I was the seventeenth!

Though a counter-intuitive proposition for some, the single most powerful and liberating realization for a leader is when they truly comprehend that the role is not about them. Authentic leadership is serving a worthwhile purpose through others and for the benefit of many. It is about making oneself less so that the ones being served might become more.

This hit home for me when I served as the chief innovation officer of a large international aid and development NGO. I had come across from the corporate world where the idea of building a legacy is often about climbing the ladder, making oneself indispensable, and accumulating credit. Now I was in a sector where this was turned completely on its head. The opposite was true. From day one of this NGO engaging with a community living in poverty, it was all about leaving. That is, the organization was very intentional about building the people up so that they were no longer dependent on external assistance, thereby restoring the health, dignity, and sustainability of the community (and freeing the NGO to move onto the next group in need). Maximum impact, minimum footprint. Sometimes that process might take ten or fifteen years, depending on the complexity of the challenges. Nevertheless, it was a process of patiently building capacity and confidence in others, day by day, one element at a time. True success is visiting one of those communities a few years later to find them utilizing all that had been developed in them and taking it to the next level themselves. This same principle should be true of any genuinely purpose-driven organization.

We have a built-in desire to make a difference, to be significant, and to be valued. Most would ideally like to make a lasting impression and have others think well of them and their contribution. This is only natural. But this desire can go one of two ways: we can seek to build either a *monument* or a *legacy*.

A monument is static and inert, like a statue or a portrait. It points to the past and is typically erected to commemorate a person. If someone else chooses to honor an exceptional leader with a monument, that's well and good. It's a nice gesture. But if we were to do that for ourselves—either literally or in the way we behave—we'd come across as somewhat narcissistic.

A legacy is quite different. It is something that lives on, pointing forward to the future. It is intended to perpetuate a purpose beyond oneself. A legacy is a gift to the next cohort of leaders and staff, a commissioning and enabling of them to go on to achieve greater things.

By setting them up for success, our contribution lives on dynamically through their endeavors, rather than statically on a wall, plinth, or pedestal. The purpose is served intergenerationally. It is the combination of our work, and those who come after us, that together realize the end goal. In that sense we're only complete together. Each contributor achieves more than they could by themselves because others' efforts build on theirs. It is in this long arc of change, this joined-upness of effort, that the lasting significance we had hoped for becomes more fully evident.

It is said that if one takes care of their character, their reputation will look after itself. So it is with legacy. We build one not by appropriating it for ourselves but rather by giving ourselves away. By serving a worthy purpose and connecting others to it. By being resolute and demonstrating integrity so that the course is stayed. And by having the humility to understand that our contribution is only a passing one unless it is joined with others in service of the same purpose. If we take care of these things, the legacy comes all by itself.

CONCLUSION

THE END OF THE BEGINNING

*"Now this is not the end. It is not even the beginning of the end.
But it is, perhaps, the end of the beginning."*

—WINSTON CHURCHILL

There's something exciting about reaching a new point of strategic clarity, that eureka moment when the perplexing suddenly becomes simpler, when the penny drops, when the fog lifts. It's exciting not because the challenge itself is any less complex than it was a minute ago, but because we now see its nub, and beyond that, a new glimmer of light. There is a sense of convergence and culmination as at the end of a long or arduous search. And yet, at the same time, it also feels like a door has opened to a new vista of possibilities. Those moments represent both the end of the beginning and the prospect of something new and wonderful. Our imagination kicks into gear once again, and we lean into the future with new confidence.

The quest for such clarity is at its most meaningful when it crystallizes our understanding of *why* we're here and what difference it makes (purpose), *how* we might best bring about the desired future (strategy), and *who* we are to those we're traveling with (leadership).

The lucidity comes from the call of something or someone greater. From seeing things in perspective. By stripping away the unnecessary, the unproductive, the peripheral, to reveal the simplicity within. By prioritizing that which is of higher value and more enduring benefit. By connecting every substantial choice and every person in our charge to the purpose we have committed to.

For any enterprise to grow in its moral, social, and financial outcomes (meaning, impact, and sustainability), it must be on the foundation of such a purpose, one that is worthy of all that it may demand of us. There is no alternative if we're seeking all three as a complete set, being unwilling to settle for less.

This in turn requires people who'll stand on that, sense its promise and possibilities, see the way ahead, and step forward into that future.

*"A leader is one who knows the way, goes the way,
and shows the way."*

—John C. Maxwell

The three dimensions we've explored in this book are the keys to operating in this way. They are complementary and necessarily go together.

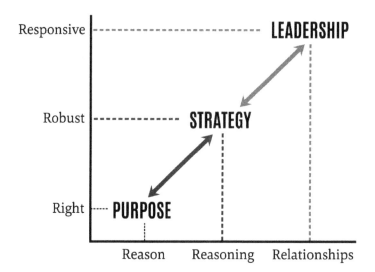

Purpose ensures we're proceeding for the *right reason*. It provides both the assurance that it's all worth it, and the consistency needed to build something meaningful over time. It is also a source of inspiration: a call upward into a higher aspiration and forward into new territory. A great purpose engages our heart as well as our head. Being so foundational it should be settled and stable and our commitment steadfast.

Strategy ensures *robust reasoning*. We cannot predict everything perfectly, but we can make choices that provide clear direction and sound logic while also leaving room to learn and adapt as we move ahead. Our strategy will evolve more often than our purpose but in a way that is still very intentional, thoughtful, and disciplined.

Leadership needs to be the most agile of all. Its consistent aim is to connect people to the purpose via the strategy. Its variability is in the wide range of stakeholders we must engage throughout the circumstances of each day. This is about building *responsive relationships*, both vertically and horizontally. The art of leadership is in making the shared purpose personal—helping everyone find their why and their way within the bigger picture. If we do that, we all grow personally, vocationally, and corporately—even through all the twists and turns of the journey.

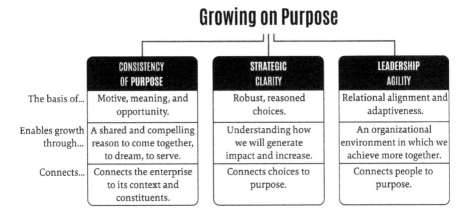

Growing on Purpose

	CONSISTENCY OF PURPOSE	STRATEGIC CLARITY	LEADERSHIP AGILITY
The basis of...	Motive, meaning, and opportunity.	Robust, reasoned choices.	Relational alignment and adaptiveness.
Enables growth through...	A shared and compelling reason to come together, to dream, to serve.	Understanding how we will generate impact and increase.	An organizational environment in which we achieve more together.
Connects...	Connects the enterprise to its context and constituents.	Connects choices to purpose.	Connects people to purpose.

Authentically purpose-driven leaders serve a cause in a way that ultimately results in impact and increase. They get the order right. They wisely gather the insights and evidence they can, but they also know where to place their faith as they navigate their way through the unknowns. They focus on the things that really matter. They find both creative freedom and professional excellence within the space bounded by their assigned role, unique gifts, and values they abide by. They put others' welfare and growth first, assured that their own will follow. They sow generously in anticipation of a rich harvest, not wanting to miss that outcome by allowing themselves to become weary or discouraged before then.

In combination, these qualities channel a kind of magnanimous power, "the strength required to bring about social, political, and economic change," as Dr. Martin Luther King Jr. put it.

The crafts of strategic thinking and leadership are developed over time. Having determined they're skills we want to acquire, we lean in and take every opportunity to apply the principles in practice. Early on, this may seem awkward at times. There will be missteps along the way, but we can be heartened by the fact that this is where most learning happens. Gradually, the pieces will fall into place, the disciplines become second nature, and the results will flow. At some stage we will look back and appreciate just how far we have come.

Consistency of purpose is of a different nature. It is not so much a craft as a choice. One that we make up-front as we decide where to invest our personal and corporate lives. It is also a commitment that must be reaffirmed at many points along the journey, particularly when the going gets tough. Some go searching for that sense of purpose, whereas for others the purpose or call seems to find them. Either way, we still make the choice as to who or what we will give ourselves to. What it is that we consider to be worthy of such investment, especially the one resource we can never reclaim: our time. This is the most profound choice of all for it determines both direction and destination, and the meaning we derive from the journey in between. All of this—everything in this book and the clarity we seek—comes down to one pivotal decision, one that will change everything that follows.

"Choose for yourselves this day whom you will serve."

—Joshua 24:15 AMP

ENDNOTES

Introduction: The Challenge

1   Martin Luther King Jr., "Where Do We Go From Here?," Address Delivered at the Eleventh Annual SCLC Convention in Atlanta, Georgia, August 16, 1967.

2   Martin Luther King Jr., "Where Do We Go From Here?," Address Delivered at the Eleventh Annual SCLC Convention in Atlanta, Georgia, August 16, 1967.

3   Source: Edelman Trust Barometer Global Report, 2019, https://www.edelman.com/sites/g/files/aatuss191/files/2019-02/2019_Edelman_Trust_Barometer_Global_Report.pdf

4   Shannon Schuyler, "Putting Purpose to Work: A study of purpose in the workplace," PwC Charitable Foundation, Inc., June 2016, https://www.pwc.com/us/en/purpose-workplace-study.html.

5   "State of the Global Workplace," Gallup, 2017, https://www.gallup.com/workplace/349484/state-of-the-global-workplace-2022-report.aspx.

6   "Global Trends Report", IPSOS, 2023. https://www.ipsos.com/en/global-trends.

7   "Purpose 2020: Igniting Purpose-Led Growth", Kantar Consulting, 2020. https://kantar.no/globalassets/ekspertiseomrader/merkevarebygging/purpose-2020/p2020-frokostseminar-250418.pdf.

8   BRAC profile on Wikipedia. https://en.wikipedia.org/wiki/BRAC_(organisation). Accessed 7 July, 2023.

9   "Confronting Complexity Research Findings and Insights", KPMG International. May 2011

10   M. Porter and N. Nohria, "How CEOs Manage Time," Harvard Business Review, July-August 2018, 9, 12.

11   Milton Friedman, *Capitalism and Freedom,* 2nd Ed. (Chicago: University of Chicago Press, September 15, 1982)

12   Louis Pasteur in a lecture delivered at the University of Lille, 7 December
      1854.

Chapter 1: Consistency of Purpose

1   Oxford Dictionary.

Chapter 2: Finding Purpose

1   Walmart website. https://corporate.walmart.com/purpose. Accessed 15 July,
      2023.
2   Karl Marx, in the introduction to, *Critique of Hegel's Philosophy of Right*
      (Cambridge: Cambridge University Press, 1843), 131.
3   Richard Dawkins, *River Out of Eden: A Darwinian View of Life* (New York:
      Basic Books, 1996).
4   Billy Graham, *The Secret of Happiness* (Nashville: Thomas Nelson Publish-
      ers, 2002).

Chapter 3: Purpose Finding You

1   Eugene H. Peterson, *A Long Obedience in the Same Direction: Discipleship in
      an Instant Society* (Downers Grove, Ill.: InterVarsity Press, 1980), quoting
      Friedrich Nietzsche.
2   Clarence Prouty Shedd, *History of the World's Alliance of Young Men's Chris-
      tian Associations* (London: SPCK, 1955).

Chapter 4: Elevate Your View

1   Laurent Chevreux, Jose Lopez, and Xavier Mesnard, The Best Companies
      Know How to Balance Strategy and Purpose," *Harvard Business Review*,
      November 2, 2017, https://hbr.org/2017/11/the-best-companies-know-
      how-to-balance-strategy-and-purpose.
2   Dorie Clarke, "If Strategy Is So Important, Why Don't We Make Time for
      It?", Harvard Business Review, June 21, 2018, https://hbr.org/2018/06/if-
      strategy-is-so-important-why-dont-we-make-time-for-it.

3   Jeanne M. Liedtka, "Strategic thinking: Can it be taught?" *Long Range
     Planning*, Volume 31, Issue 1, February 1998, Pages 120-129.

4   Howard H. Stevenson, "The Heart of Entrepreneurship," *Harvard Business
     Review*, March 1985, https://hbr.org/2013/01/what-is-entrepreneurship?

Chapter 5: Frame the Opportunity

1   Theodore Levitt, "Marketing Myopia," *Harvard Business Review*, July-Au-
     gust 1960, 45-46.

2   Here I use the term "vision" in its broadest sense, meaning a picture of the
     desired future or outcome we're seeking to bring about. Certainly, it refers
     to the long-range corporate vision. But it can also apply to a mid-term
     milestone in that direction (e.g., a five-year strategic intent, for example).

Chapter 6: Identify the Turning Points

1   Keeping in mind that the organization's purpose should ideally remain
     consistent in most cases (and to a lesser extent, the vision should as well)
     because they are the basis of organizational meaning and direction there's
     value in stability here.

Chapter 7: Connect the Dots

1   "Music." Merriam-Webster.com Dictionary, Merriam-Webster, https://
     www.merriam-webster.com/dictionary/music. Accessed 18 Jan. 2023.

Part III: Leadership Agility

1   All the management tasks (such as administering resources, finances, pro-
     cesses, and systems) are also critically important. To draw the distinction
     with leadership is not to undervalue them. But they are in a different cate-
     gory for they are inanimate in themselves, playing a supporting role. They
     are instruments we utilise to enable *people* to collectively pursue a shared
     purpose.

Chapter 8: Connect People to Purpose

1   "The Advantages of Employee Care: Creating Human-Centric Employee Experiences and Work Environments," Metlife 20th Annual U.S. Employee Benefit Trends Study, 2022, https://www.metlife.com/employee-benefit-trends/2022-employee-benefit-trends/.

2   Boris Groysberg, Jeremiah Lee, Jesse Price, J. Yo-Jud Cheng, "The Leader's Guide to Corporate Culture." *Harvard Business Review,* January-February 2018, https://hbr.org/2018/01/the-leaders-guide-to-corporate-culture.

3   Luke 6:45

4   Adapted from an address by Mathew Stevenson, Edge Church International, 2022.

Chapter 10: Serve the Purpose

1   David Brooks, "The Moral Bucket List," *New York Times*, April 11, 2015, https://www.nytimes.com/2015/04/12/opinion/sunday/david-brooks-the-moral-bucket-list.html.

INDEX

A

abolition of slavery, 40, 71
Adams, John Quincy, 190
adaptable choice, 138
Amazon, 109
Amnesty International, 117
Angelou, Maya, 208
answers, provisional, 140
Apple, 40, 103, 109
Archimedes, 14

B

Bacon, Francis, 71, 126
Bennis, Warren, 13
Bezos, Jeff, 185
Bonaparte, Napoleon, 110
Booth, Catherine, 70
BRAC (Bangladeshi nonprofit), 4–5
Brooks, David (*NYT*), 200–201

C

calling. *See chapter 3, "Purpose Finding You"* (69–74)
    the impact of Christians with a sense of, 71
Carter, Jimmy, 73

D

E

F

G

K

L

M

N

O

T

U

V

W

Milton Keynes UK
Ingram Content Group UK Ltd.
UKHW022128201123
432954UK00014B/564/J